MW00479294

MENDING MESOPOTAMIA

The Gospel and Healing in Iraq

MENDING MESOPOTAMIA

The Gospel and Healing in Iraq

MARK A. WEHLE

Cover design by Steven Novak

Interior print design and layout by Sydnee K. Hyer

Ebook design and layout by Sydnee K. Hyer

Published by WehleFamily Press

978-0-578-39493-0

FOREWORD

Mark was born February 15, 1959, in the District of Columbia to Kurt and Ednamae Wiese Wehle. He was the youngest of four children. He graduated from high school in 1977. In 1978, his mother passed away from cancer at fifty-nine, after which Mark chose to join the Navy Engineering Division, known as the Seabees, in February 1979. He was honorably discharged in 1984. During his experience in the Navy, he met a few members of The Church of Jesus Christ of Latter-day Saints, including Pat Crowley and Michael Remillard. These two Navy buddies had a great influence on him; Mark was impressed by their devotion and belief and began to ponder about religion. Joining the Church was a decision he did not take lightly. Although he needed to make a few changes in his life to live by his newfound knowledge, he would often positively share the stories of his conversion and his gratitude for having found the truth of the restored gospel of Jesus Christ.

Mark married Sharon Worrell (me) on June 28, 1986, in the Mesa, Arizona temple of The Church of Jesus Christ of Latter-Day Saints. He graduated from Brigham Young University with a BS in mechanical engineering. While pursuing his undergraduate degree, he and I welcomed two little boys, David James and Matthew Allen, into our family. After accepting employment with General Electric, we moved to Virginia, where we had two more children, Cherie Elizabeth and Jonathan Michael. We lived in Bumpass, VA, in a log cabin-style home with less than one thousand sq. ft. Mark would be called as the bishop of the Scotchtown Ward, Richmond Stake, at the ripe old age of thirty-five, and it was a wonderful experience of enrichment and growth for him and the entire family. In 2000, we would buy 7½ acres and build a beautiful home in Stafford, VA, with all four children still under twelve years old.

Sadly, the date of his marriage would also be the very day he left this Earth and returned to his Heavenly Father. He passed away on a business trip with what we believe to be a heart attack in Marietta, Georgia, on Monday, June 28, 2010, at fifty-one years old.

Mark's journal entries provide a powerful witness of his conversion to the restored gospel of Jesus Christ:

> I would end up going to Guam for an 8 month stay, having a Church member move in the barracks where I was, and I started learning about the Church. A missionary couple (Pop & Berna Davies of Fillmore, Utah) became assigned to the area and I took the missionary discussions there in Guam with them. The couple was special and something connected. I was hit with a ton of bricks that the Church is true, and that sweet feeling come over me that I needed to join and be baptized. I found out later that my Navy buddies and Brother & Sister Davies had been fasting for me that night. We know

the spirit protects us in many ways, even as a non-member. I feel that Heavenly Father knows us so well that he knew I needed that opportunity at conversion without the distraction of a spouse, or steady girlfriend affecting my judgment and my reception to the promptings of the Holy Ghost. In my conversion I had the Spirit strongly overcome me one evening out in the jungle in Guam. It told me 3 distinct things: 1) that these were His people, and I was to come join them; 2) that I had responsibilities to live up to in this life; 3) and that there were other beings dependent on me (whether dead, alive or pre-mortal—I don't know).

I am a true convert to the Church. I wasn't born into the Church, and I didn't join because of a girl. I was converted by missionaries who prayed and fasted for me, and the Spirit answered those prayers with a strong witness to me of what I was expected to do for myself and my Heavenly Father and His Son, Jesus Christ.

Mark and I met at a Church dance for single adults in Virginia soon after he was released from the Navy. At the right time, Mark would retrieve his mother's ring from his father, who was keeping it safe for him, and ask me to marry him for not just time but for all eternity.

At nineteen years old, right before Mark's mother passed, she pulled Mark to her bedside, put her left hand out to grab him, and said, "Someday, you will meet a nice girl, and I want you to give her this ring." Mark wrote about this experience in his journal:

My mother giving me that ring taught me a most valuable principle. And in or out of the Church this principle applies throughout cultures. That unions are sacred, and it is truly a union of families. There are eternal principles involved that we might not understand. Many people are involved and affected by the choices we make, and marriage predominates as the most life changing decision we must decide.

Just as Satan places obstacles in front of us, Heavenly Father provides escape routes. Sometimes these escape routes can even look like you and me. We are instruments in the hands of Heavenly Father to reach out to others, love them, help them, and comfort them. It can be a heavy weight, but we are to "bear one another's burdens" (Mosiah 18:8). This support can be provided in many ways. The emotional support and common-sense advice we give to others is a critical role we play as Church members and children of our Heavenly Father. This effort is something we engage in for the rest of our lives.

For me, too, our marriage was the most life-changing decision we ever decided together. It brought us the most life-changing joy as well. I'm grateful for my time with Mark, and I'm also grateful for the spirit of love he was able to share with our spiritual brothers and sisters all over the Earth.

—SHARON E. WEHLE, AUTHOR'S WIFE

PREFACE

I n the summer of 2004, my father, Mark Wehle, flew across the world to help bring electricity back to the people of Iraq. Even though I was a typical, self-absorbed high schooler at the time, I could tell this particular trip was different. It was an incredibly spiritual experience for him, almost like the Latter-day Saint mission he never got to serve (he was an active member of the Navy when he was baptized in Guam at nineteen). After he returned, Iraq was all he talked about. Strangely enough to me, he always mentioned how much he loved the people there. At the time, I couldn't wrap my mind around loving an entire group of people, but I saw glimpses of that love. At one point, our phone rang every other day, and every time one of us would pick it up, we'd hear some broken English variation of "Hello, Mr. Mark, this is Galib. We love you. We miss you." My dad would often talk to them, and the excitement in his voice was palpable. When my dad was away, I'd try to let the callers know in simple words that my dad loved them too and that he hoped to see them again. He truly missed his friends from the ancient lands of Mesopotamia.

In June 2010, my dad unexpectedly passed away from a heart attack. He was fifty-one. It broke our hearts and spirits in a lot of ways, and we are still healing from the void he left in our lives. However, we are grateful for the remarkable impact he had on us as an incredible father and husband. During the funeral, one of my dad's close friends mentioned the book he was working on about his experiences in Iraq and how I would be the one to finish it. No problem, I thought. I would have plenty of time!

No one seemed to warn me that adulthood and parenthood came with a complete dissipation of free time. I met the love of my life, we had children, I focused on building my career, and before I knew it, ten years had passed. To this day, I still feel guilty about how long it took to finish this book. It was always hovering in the back of my mind, probably due to some promptings from beyond the veil. I can't stress how important this work was to my dad. This book is the legacy he wanted to share with the world for generations to come.

Right before my mission, my dad would excitedly share with me early chapters. We were supposed to be doing church lessons together to prepare me to enter the temple for the first time, but I think he was too excited. We would brainstorm the best ways to lay out his experiences and engage the reader. He kept saying he wanted this book to be the kind you can't put down after you start. He would tell me in detail about the roadside bombs and the people tragically killed, and he would ask me not to tell Mom, so that she wouldn't worry too much (sorry, Mom).

He went back and forth on the title. For a while, the book was titled "A Noble Cause," and then later, he wanted to add the subtitle "Why I Went Back." That's because my dad made two separate, monumental trips to Iraq: the first in 2004 to Basra just outside Kuwait and the second in 2007 just outside Baghdad. Each trip lasted around four to six months, with a Christmas break in the middle when he flew home for a few weeks. Originally my dad wanted to write in-depth about both of his trips, but he only finished the first half before his passing. I have done my best to conclude his 2007 journey using letters and journal entries.

My dad eventually settled on the title *Mending Mesopotamia* because not only was he helping mend the electrical infrastructure, but he was also preaching the restored gospel to the children of Abraham. He was a humble servant: he didn't speak Arabic, he legally wasn't allowed to preach his beliefs to the Muslim populace, and he was a busy engineer with the burden of an entire power plant on his shoulders, but he still found time to bond with the good people there and to love them unconditionally.

A prophet named Alma from the Book of Mormon taught this unforgettable principle to his son: "Behold I say unto you, that by small and simple things are great things brought to pass; and small means in many instances doth confound the wise. And the Lord God doth work by means to bring about his great and eternal purposes; and by very small means the Lord doth confound the wise and bringeth about the salvation of many souls" (Alma 37:6–7).

It is my testimony that my father did a great many small things in the land of Iraq pertaining to sharing the gospel and to showing charity to all Heavenly Father's children, and I know he is doing the same thing now with the spirits who have passed on from this Earth. Please share my father's record with all you know, so that the Lord's work, which is the "stone [that] was cut out without hands," will continue to roll forth and fill the whole earth (Daniel 2:34–35).

—DAVID WEHLE, AUTHOR'S SON

INTRODUCTION

I just didn't know what to truly expect. Nor did I ever antici-pate I would eventually end up as a leading American techni-cal representative located on the project site of one of the largest, US taxpayer-funded power generation projects in Iraq. I would become one of a small population of American workers that would spend the bulk of my time shoulder to shoulder with Iraqi citizens, working hand-in-hand with them as I learned much about their culture and their language and was privy to their daily discussions, thoughts, and emotions.

I witnessed many of the major news headlines through-out this period at some unique vantage point: the events lead-ing up to the first Iraqi elections, the first address of an Iraqi prime minister to the US Congress, the assault on Fallujah, the Baghdad troop surge, the hanging of Saddam, the resurgence of the Muqtada al-Sadr militia. All these were first-hand events to me.

All in all, I spent over twenty-four months working, living, eating, and sleeping under the skies of Iraq. I met and worked with dozens of their citizens, many US and UK troops, and government leaders all engaged in putting electrical power back into Iraqi homes and businesses.

In this book, you will find my record of this time and how I worked with the people of Iraq to bring them necessary electrical power. You'll also see how the people and their godly kindness and humility were the most integral part of my experience. I hope my words properly convey the impact these people had on me, and perhaps can also have on you.

Please note that names have been changed to protect identities and to keep people safe.

CHAPTER 1

Standing in the cold Wisconsin wind in 2006, I listened to a deep, Texas voice on my cell phone explain a new mission while memories of my 2004 assignment were summoned by his words, "Go back to Iraq." It shifted me into another mental zone. So, I told him I would call back that night from my motel room. I was out of town at a client's power plant looking over some maintenance guidelines while simultaneously trying to answer a slew of emails. When I went back into the plant's control room, I was mentally detached, and my mind went back to September 2004…

I never expected to experience the strength of a roadside bomb. Most of us have seen a Hollywood explosion in a movie or on TV. Loud, booming bass, bright lights. It's not the same. Instantaneously, the force and concussion penetrate throughout your body. You have no idea what's going on, who's been struck. Fear and uncertainty grip your heart while you wonder if your vehicle will be next.

That Iraqi day was calm as we headed away from one of Saddam Hussein's aging power plants near Basra in an armored vehicle team of three. But serenity was replaced by shock, fright, and worry. Without warning, the explosion and resultant concussion rocked our vehicle, and an immediate cloud of dust turned the southern Iraqi morning into a thick, eerie fog that shrouded our vehicle team in blindness. The private security team driver of our vehicle reacted instantly after the initial stun of the blast, his front-seat lookout shouting "GO! GO! GO!" into the communications radio for all vehicles in our team to take action. Since we were the second vehicle in the team, it wasn't immediately known to us if the Improvised Explosive Device (IED) had hit the first vehicle or not.

At that instant, there was a risk of us crashing into that front vehicle as we began blindly charging through the heavy dust. Our security men had to make a split-second decision which turned out to be correct. Neither vehicle was hit by the weapon. The lead vehicle reacted to the radio command, and all vehicles were racing through the thick dust on these dusty roads within moments of the explosion. The deafening ringing in my ears muffled most of the action. It all happened fast.

My Pakistani colleague, Ikram, and myself were the only "clients" in the rear seat of the vehicle on this occasion. Somewhat immovable due to the thick, body-armor vests we were required to wear, we both managed to clasp our hands together tightly, hold a breath, then bow our heads while we closed our eyes tightly as in a prayer. Neither of us were ashamed to show a little fear and court heaven for deliverance.

Radio traffic went wild. Our security team rushed the vehicle convoy out of the area, raising a cloud of dust that left the third vehicle virtually navigating the roads blindfolded. We drove on the brink of control back onto hard paved roads and, in a roundabout fashion, through the town of Az Zubayr outside of Basra. Quickly, we returned to the safety of our contractor camp located inside the British-controlled Coalition base named Shaibah Logistic Base.

In our case, only small fragments of shrapnel had hit our vehicle, cracked the windshield, and did some undercarriage damage that was discovered later. Timing is key to the success or failure of these explosive devices. We were fortunate to have had some distance between the bomb and us, and we had the ability to drive away. In this attack the IED missed its target, which was most likely any random coalition force vehicle that happened by. We weren't sure if it was planted specifically for any contractor team working on the power plant equipment in the area. Unfortunately, the private security teams and military teams sometimes were indistinguishable by the vehicles each team drove.

My ears continued ringing well into that night, but even worse was the overall demoralizing effect of the explosion, which was substantial. We would end up being in a lockdown status in our contractor camp for a total of four days. Visualize four days of shaken men continually talking about the event, speculating and theorizing. Sort of like gossip where the story goes around and around, the perception of the event was getting skewed. Fear took its toll, and there was the beginning of an unfounded mistrust of our private security company. Were they forthright with all the information they were receiving after the event? Were corporate forces at work to console us and keep us on the job? If contractors leave, then security contractors have no task to perform and are unemployed. It was a complex arena of circumstances.

Amidst all the discussion that took place with our security contractors those next few days, our team specifically stressed to us to always be alert along with them. More eyes were always welcome, we were told. And these security teams were conditioned to avoid callous attitudes toward our observations. Things to look for included parked, late-model cars where perpetrators could position themselves for device detonation as we neared the "kill zone."

We were accustomed to the children running up to the road and giving the thumbs up to us as we drove by on a daily basis. It made me feel good. These security men explained to us that it's possible for local children to sometimes give a thumbs down as a warning that suspicious activity has taken place. Our team leader detailed a specific account of this event that had taken place earlier in the year with one private security team operating north of Baghdad in unfamiliar territory. Kids were running up and giving the thumbs down to them. Being new to this area, this private security team just thought these kids were rude. As they continued along their route, they were narrowly missed by an IED a short distance away. After consulting with counterpart security teams familiar to that area, they discovered the children had been giving them the warning sign. It was a common communication tool used between the locals and the Coalition forces and contractor teams.

In other areas of the country, Coalition forces and private security teams noticed the adults avoided eye contact if insurgents were around. When the coast was clear, it was back to smiles, waves, and friendly eye contact as the Western security teams would drive through. This was just one of several remarkable pieces of information our security contractors would eventually relay to us throughout my time in Iraq.

But the veracity of this event was unshakable. A bomb went off that could have killed or maimed any of us. It was a lesson in reality that all Iraq is dangerous and none of us could be complacent about security measures. We were all free to leave at any time, and discussion was rampant throughout our team about doing so. One engineer from each of the two projects I was involved with decided to quit and go home. The blessing was that we had survived this IED contact event. Fortunately, it was a miss.

I spent the next four days brooding over the situation in intense, personal reflection. Thoughts of my family back home filled my mind. How did I ever rationalize going to Iraq as a contractor in the first place? Now I faced a dilemma: to stay or go in the face of this life-threatening event. I had supposed that Basra was calm, had convinced my family of this fact, and was sure that any risk would be minimal. When that bomb went off in September 2004, I had only been in Iraq for nine days.

And now it's October of 2006, and I was again being asked to go to Iraq. The little info I made out from this initial phone call was that the location would start off in the Baghdad area. That was where the critical need was. I discussed my potential return with friends and strangers alike, so I knew what I was getting myself back into after a year and a half. With all these thoughts running through my head at the time, a dominant theme surfaced. In Iraqi Arabic, I was thinking the word *mijnoon* to myself. It means "crazy."

CHAPTER 2

So, how did I ever get to be one of the few to make my way to Iraq and support a broken nation in the first place? And how does a father of four get his wife and children on board and calm their concerns? Maybe it goes back to the roots of a person.

In the earliest days that I can recall, I was one who would eagerly disassemble a brand-new BB gun or try to determine how a toy truck would propel itself after being wound up. Teenage years found me taking a vocational education curriculum, tinkering with cars and motorcycles, and finding a little mischief where possible. The early death of my mother funneled me into a Navy enlistment shortly after my high school years in the late seventies, a path that would eventually prove beneficial. I had selected training to be a construction equipment mechanic in a Navy Seabee Battalion. This choice began my entry into the world of industrial machinery maintenance and repair.

For a young lad who just lost his mother, this change of environment was a fresh breath in a difficult phase of life. In the military ranks, I quickly learned about the world of work, responsibility, and discipline. These years also taught me skills dealing with complex mechanical equipment, civil construction (which is the Seabee mission), and exposure to a variety of people and cultures that would shape my social abilities throughout my life.

In pursuit of spiritual truth, I was led to the waters of baptism into The Church of Jesus Christ of Latter-day Saints at the age of twenty-three, shortly before the end of my five-year Navy enlistment. I became determined to pursue marriage and further my education in whatever manner possible after the honorable discharge was granted. Returning home after this time away from home allowed me to foster a better relationship with my aging father, spend time with my three older siblings, and participate in a fruitful church social life, which resulted in marriage to Sharon, my best friend and eternal companion.

As the son of a career civil service engineer in the federal government, stories of Sputnik and other engineering milestones were common discussion between my father and me throughout the years. The goal of earning a mechanical engineering degree at Brigham Young University appeared to be a good match and an appropriate step to a successful professional life after these developing years I spent in the Navy.

Three years, two children, and one bachelor's degree later, a job offer from General Electric came directly from the BYU Placement Center on the heels of graduation in the summer of 1990. It would move us to Richmond, Virginia, and land me in the heart of the power-generation industry. After some generic training and on-the-job experience, I would become one of a tight community of specialized professionals who know the intricate details of specific natural gas-fired turbines and their generators used in worldwide power-generation applications.

These large machines made by GE and others are a critical part of the core of electricity production used throughout the world. I became a field engineer, the "boots on the ground" person. My specific task would be to supply technical direction for an electric utility's labor force in the specific procedures of factory-approved inspection and repair of the gas turbine and the associated equipment. For several years I provided project management and oversight pertaining to the proper disassembly and assembly of every small and large mechanical component related to these turbine and generator sets.

Two more children would find their way into our family as I accumulated work experience and developed a management style particular for working with people and machinery. Church demands found me serving as one of the youngest bishops in the Richmond, Virginia Stake. This time in my life helped me refine my testimony, put my interpersonal skills to the test, and helped me further develop a leadership style.

After several more years from my start with GE, changes in business practices of the industry pushed me into the category of a contractor. In the corporate world, this basically translates to accepting work on a per-contract or per-job basis. My new employer, Granite Services, Inc., a subsidiary of GE, was set up to supply a variable labor force of professionals with skill sets such as mine as contractors to GE and other large corporations involved in power generation.

Work schedules for me would become seasonal in nature. When domestic electrical load is at low levels during the spring and fall, I would be busy and away from home for weeks at a time. Selected turbine and generator sets are removed from service while mandatory yearly maintenance for these massive machines is performed within the tightest schedules possible. Grueling projects that worked at a pace of two, twelve-hour shifts every workday and pressed non-stop throughout each specific maintenance project was the norm. Getting this valuable equipment back into service is critical and does not allow time for days of rest.

Some of my assignments took me outside the United States to South America, Italy, and even a trip to a failed Enron plant in India at one time. These demanding work schedules would abruptly end, and then I would find myself enjoying relaxing periods of time at home for weeks and weeks in a row during the off season. This would effectively give me the entire summer and winter to enjoy at home in a non-working status. Blocks of time spent with family in recreational pursuits, church and scouting activities, and yard work compensated for my extended absences. As a family, we adjusted to this lifestyle and would anxiously await for the commencement of the off season.

Following the domestic power plant construction boom that began in 1998 and ended sometime in 2003, I watched as oversight managers scrambled and began the musical chairs' game of job changing within our organization. Several of our clients, including GE, were going through similar acrobatics. These changes resulted in the loss of management contacts that assigned me to clients I'd been accustomed to working with throughout the years. As the 2004 spring work season concluded, I wasn't interested in investing time and lobbying the new personalities for future work. The work season had come to an end and I, just wanted my time off for the summer. Family fun had begun with the start of summer vacation.

With school and early morning seminary schedules completed, our older boys David and Matthew were ready for skateboarding, swimming, and sleeping late. Cherie, our lone girl, was anxious to start girls camp and beach vacation. And Jonathan, the youngest, was ready for trampoline time and some motorcycle riding with Dad in our large yard deep in the Virginia suburbs of Washington, DC. A few quick checks of my company email account during the summer would keep me informed as to what was available for work in the fall.

I was caught off guard when a brief "All Hands" email message came through in early June. The shock of seeing "Volunteers for Iraq work" in the subject line of this email just plain stunned me. *We really are in there*, I thought. The very company I work for was now inside Iraq and seeking additional volunteers for assignments there.

Contracts had been signed by GE with the Army Corps of Engineers, and power generation equipment that many of us were familiar with was scheduled for repairs in several areas throughout the country. Explanations detailing increased pay scales and the competency of London-based Olive Security as the private security contractor for these projects were included.

Crazy as that email appeared to me at first, it stuck in my mind for several days. To purge myself of the subject, I finally braved mention of this opportunity to my wife. I waited for the raised eyebrow and her inquiry back to me of my current state of sanity. But that anticipated scene did not play out. Actually, deep down, I think we both felt something unusual and calm about the entire scenario. The pay scale uplift was 70 percent, which I thought was kind of low for the risk. At that time, shocking media reports of contractors being killed in Iraq almost seemed like a daily occurrence. But both Sharon and I felt like Scarlet O'Hara: we would just worry about that tomorrow. For now, we had family time and summer schedules to occupy ourselves. Work worries would have to come later.

But over the weeks, I pondered about working in Iraq. What would it be like? Who would be performing the hands-on labor? Why were we rebuilding their equipment? Was it destroyed in the invasion, and am I paying for this as an American taxpayer? In the midst of these thoughts, I received an email from a close colleague named Bruce. He'd taken the plunge and had been working in Iraq for a few months already. He described a different scene than I had imagined.

Bruce removed some of the uncertainty in my mind and made it easier for me to envision myself working there. We began to have family discussions on the subject, and it was included in every family prayer from that point forward. More emails would come, and these corporate communications ensured us that we knew the assignments were entirely voluntary. Anyone assigned in Iraq could leave at any time without justification and without career penalty. So, I reasoned with myself and the rest of the family that I could just go to Iraq and return if the picture wasn't right.

Unfortunately, things changed when two distant colleagues, Bill Hoke and Raul Flores, along with two Olive Security contractors, were killed by a Baghdad car bomb in June. The event made the national media rounds. A third Granite employee identified only as a Frenchman was killed in the attack also, but he was never named publicly. While I didn't know Bill and Raul personally, the shock put the thought of working in Iraq in canceled mode in my mind. Instead, I focused in on the family schedule and fulfilling my summer volunteer obligations for all the Church activities that were going on.

But emails and pictures kept coming from Bruce working in the southern region. He had also braved work in treacherous areas near Baghdad and Taji for a few weeks. The work atmosphere of the Shiite south he described was starting to sound attractive. By the latter part of the summer, feedback from company management was hinting that the upcoming fall work season might be slow, which I suspected, and Iraq work and the financial rewards were looking tempting to me.

Sharon and I drew on prayer, my inside information, and common sense with faith in divine help in making the proper decision. There was never a feeling of impending doom or any natural inclinations to scrap the entire idea. It was just one of those things that we felt okay about. The children were basically indifferent on the subject and, as typical kids, were not paying attention to media reports the way we adults were. Without much apprehension, we decided I would go. It was late August.

But once the decision was made, I felt like a child getting the nerve to go off the high dive for the first time. I had butterflies in my stomach I couldn't seem to get rid of. My employer was pleased I had volunteered and assured me I'd be in good hands with Olive Security once I was in the Middle East. In a relatively quiet manner, I slipped down to United States Central Command (CENTCOM) at MacDill Air Force Base in Florida for screening and documentation while the mobilization strategy was being finalized by Granite Services. I invited the bishop to come over and give me a blessing that next Sunday even as I downplayed the entire assignment to him. It was the last Sunday in August, and I would be off to Iraq the next day, flying into Kuwait City via London from DC. The blessing helped, but the butterflies never left.

Tears, kisses, and hugs escorted me to the terminal at Dulles Airport where my pioneer-spirited wife took charge of the family and put trust in her faith that I would be back alive and well when the project was over. The long, drowsy commercial flight to Kuwait via London conditioned my mental state for a groggy entrance into the Islamic world. When the plane touched down at dawn and I stepped out onto the scorching earth, I knew distinctly I was in another culture mixed with pieces of my own.

I sheepishly avoided eye contact to show respect and reverence in the Kuwait airport by not staring at veiled women, as well as men dressed in traditional Arab garb. There were enough Westerners walking throughout the terminal that I wasn't totally out of place. After collecting my belongings and clearing customs, an Olive Security employee intercepted me in the terminal and escorted me outside to load the vehicle. The heat, humidity, and somewhat ocean-tainted smell surprised me that morning. Even though it was still early, it was probably in the high nineties. My Olive Security escort drove me to an upscale hotel in Kuwait City where I immediately fell into the bed to recover from my jetlag for a few hours. When I awoke, I took a cab into town for some last-minute shopping. The heat was stifling. Without a doubt, I was on the other side of the world.

I was assigned to work in the far southern sector below the famous Sunni Triangle, but firmly in the Shiite-dominated region of the country near Basra. In my case, I was offered to GE to assist in the refurbishment of one of the four natural-gas–fired turbine and generator sets located at the Basra petrochemical complex known as PC-1.

Designed and built by the British in the late 1970s, this was one of the many US Army Corps of Engineers electrical generation restoration projects throughout Iraq. It was also one of the earliest contracts signed with Western companies after the toppling of the Saddam regime. The contractor camp we would be staying at was located on the ex-Iraqi military airfield known as Shaibah, now controlled by the British military and designated as Shaibah Logistic Base. Olive Security would have overall charge of my food, housing, safety, and transportation once I arrived in Kuwait.

CHAPTER 3

Kuwait is well known as the gateway into southern Iraq. It is a small, modern country and very Western-influenced in regard to their infrastructure, architecture, commerce, and societal attitude. The government is a constitutional monarchy and has been going through some democratic reforms. They are pro-Western and still grateful for the US intervention we know as Desert Storm. This was the famous Gulf War that liberated the people of Kuwait from the seven-month Iraqi occupation that began in August 1990.

The major religion is Islam; however, there is tolerance toward other faiths. English is spoken frequently, and a few Christian churches can be found scattered among the mosques throughout Kuwait City, the capital. Road signs and shopping stores are posted in Arabic as well as the English interpretation. Loud speakers faithfully blare out the morning and midday prayers from the mosques, as well as the concluding round at sunset. There is no alcohol allowed in the country.

Oil revenues have had the effect of modernizing the country, distributing wealth to the native Kuwaitis and sustaining a flourishing society of expatriates who perform the services demanded by the population. The native Kuwaitis make up approximately 37 percent of the population. It is not unusual to walk throughout the streets of Kuwait City on a typical day and see people from India, Pakistan, Bangladesh, Egypt, Lebanon, Indonesia, Malaysia, the Philippines, as well as Europeans and Americans, and yet not cross paths with a native Kuwaiti for several hours.

The standard amenities of Western society are found there. Food franchises, gasoline stations, shopping malls, plush hotels, late-model vehicles, and plenty of traffic jams ignite reminders of life at home. Westerners walk freely throughout Kuwait City, and the danger is assessed as low by the US Department of State. Western women aren't required to be veiled, and many of the Muslim women have taken on a somewhat trendy style of fashionable attire while still maintaining the Islamic standards of modesty. It seemed to be an orderly and docile society. But why would I spend time extolling the virtues and present-day make-up of Kuwait? Simply because of the stark contrast that was about to follow.

I would get to spend only three days in this glamorous hotel in Kuwait, enjoying Arabic and English cable TV, a high-speed internet connection, and top-of-the-line gourmet food. Frankly, I was somewhat nervous about being in an Islamic country, so I didn't venture much outside the hotel room after my initial shopping trip. Media from home had me on edge, and the heat wasn't helping either.

But reality set in when the very British Olive Security contractor met me in the lobby that second evening and we went to a secluded room for the security briefing. We went through a

PowerPoint presentation that took about twenty minutes. The major types of weapons and munitions found in Iraq were displayed in close-up photos, along with the most recent threat assessments and an explanation of the different types of insurgent activity that were taking place.

Explanations of how we would be driving up through southern Iraq to our destination were detailed out for my benefit. Some basic emergency procedures were explained, and personal protective requirements established. At the end of the presentation, he produced a corporate form for me to sign indicating I had received the training. As I put my pen on the paper, I noticed the last signature was that of Bill Hoke, one of the workers killed in the Baghdad car bomb attack in June. It was quite a disturbing thing for me to see his name there, and I hesitated a moment before signing my name right below his. I slept uneasily that night while thoughts of home, family, and the soberness of mortality twisted and turned in my head for hours and hours. I wondered what I had gotten myself into.

That next day we loaded up shortly before noon, and off I went, traveling from Kuwait City to the Iraqi border town of Safwan. The ride was on a modern, four-lane highway that could rival any decent stretch of interstate in the US. It was a busy road with a few smooth, sweeping turns winding through long stretches of basically flat, uninhabited desert. There was one short uphill grade with sand-dune-type terrain along the way.

Out in the distance, small mesas, some with white rock formations tumbling into sand-swept drifts below, appeared to float on the horizon. Clusters of low, sparse vegetation dotted the landscape along with bright, pebble-sized rocks scattered about every so often. The searing heat and the overall nakedness of the bright, snow-blinding, open desert reminded me of just how fragile we are against the powerful elements of the earth. Thoughts concerning our dependency on modern conveniences ran through my mind several times.

In the distance I could see many power lines, a satellite-tower complex, small herds of camels grazing, and a few turn-offs that dead-ended at small, fenced-in facilities supporting the oil well infrastructure. There were no advertisement billboards, except for one or two small postings on the outskirts of Kuwait City that said, in English, "Explore Islam," then gave a website at the bottom. *Interesting,* I thought, *an Islamic missionary message.*

Convoys of military equipment and tanker trucks traveled in both directions. A steady stream of these tanker trucks, SUVs, late-model sports cars, and tractor-trailer rigs hauling large storage containers headed toward the Iraq border. This is the same highway that was the escape route of the Iraqi army in 1991 during their retreat from the Kuwait occupation. According to media reports of that day, this highway was bombed and littered with the bodies and equipment of the retreating forces. Looking at it at this time, one would never have guessed such death and destruction ever occurred along this stretch of road.

People were driving interstate-style, so everything moved fast. About thirty or forty minutes into the drive there was a turn-off sign for "Mutla' a Ranch," written in English and Arabic. Mounted on top of that sign was a smaller sign with bold letters on a yellow background that said, in English only, "God Bless U.S. Troops." Whether this was a privately sponsored sign, much as we see "Jesus Saves" messages throughout the US, or a state sign put in place by the Kuwaiti Transportation Authority, I never found out. I do know it has been there since before Operation Iraqi Freedom and could possibly have been put there after Desert Storm in 1991. To me, it seemed like a public message from the Kuwait people, thanking US troops for their service and sacrifice during Desert Storm, as well as a send-off message to current troops entering Iraq again, saying, "Our prayers are with you." Regardless of its origin, it demonstrated to me that there is gratitude in Kuwait, and it made me feel proud to be an American.

Not far ahead was the DMZ, or "demilitarized zone," which was established by the UN after Desert Storm. It extends three miles into Kuwait and six miles into Iraq. From the distance I could see the barbed-wire fence rolls on top of long, earthen berms that clearly delineated each side. My Olive Security escort commented that the Iraqi side was packed full of land mines after Desert Storm, but he didn't know the current status.

The Kuwait side of the border looked like one huge interstate truck stop. Rows and rows of tractor-trailers lined parking areas waiting for loads or clearances and lining up to rendezvous with their military or private security escorts. It was an amazing sight to see the magnitude of the supply chain that feeds the military and rebuilding efforts through this section of the country. Many of the trucks were tankers carrying fresh water. After experiencing the brutal heat of the region, I realized how critical the transportation of water is to the entire effort. It impressed upon me the reality that fresh water is truly the lifeblood of the earth.

We pass through a couple checkpoints manned by British and US forces that required proper documentation, then a final Kuwaiti checkpoint with Kuwait army guards and that was it. We were granted access into Iraq and were near the town of Safwan. I could see buildings not too far away. An Iraqi border entry to check in and present documents to Iraqi authorities did not exist. My Olive Security escort explained that because of the regime change and the steep level of corruption in the past, it could be quite a while until the new government would administrate their borders. Commenting further, he said it would not be out of line to speculate that if Iraqis were at the border crossing points this soon after the regime overthrow, corruption could still play a role in further hampering the rebuild activity taking place in our region. "After all," he said, "we have a price on our heads."

CHAPTER 4

When heading into Iraq as a civilian worker, the protocol seems to be that the private security companies have total charge of getting contractors to the border, as well as keeping those contractors under their authority and protection full-time once inside. After crossing over, there was no visible military support for us other than some communications between the Olive teams and military units. I felt that I was in good hands with Olive. However, we were somewhat separate from the military organizations that we had seen so far. Basically, we were on our own.

For the trip from Kuwait City, my Olive Security escort used a "soft" vehicle, which meant the vehicle was not fitted with the special, thick, metal plating and bulletproof windows that make up an armored vehicle. Once across the border, we promptly pulled off onto a packed sand parking area for the transfer to "hard" vehicles and armed guards. I couldn't help but notice all the litter on the ground. Empty water bottles and paper refuse could be seen everywhere. We were only a couple hundred yards into Iraq, and already it was visibly different than the Kuwait side.

Our armed security team from Olive was there and ready to make the transfer. I was given a heavy body armor vest and helmet. Stern instructions were repeated that unless an Olive Security team member gave me clearance to remove them, the helmet and vest were to be worn at all times. The bulky vest and clumsy helmet were considered as critical a piece of equipment for me as the weapons were to the Olive men. No contractors were to carry weapons.

The physical appearance of the Olive Security team on this side of the border was impressive. All were of Caucasian descent, being from the UK, Ireland, Australia, and South Africa. Most had a Special Forces or UK Royal Marine background and several had been to Iraq in previous military campaigns at one time or another. They were all in good physical condition, carried AK-47s, and wore a lean form of black body armor vests while sporting celebrity-type Ray-Ban shades. The uniformity of their appearance was unique depending on their national origin.

For the UK, Australian, and Irish nationals, standard grooming seemed to be skinhead-style haircuts and clean-shaven faces. Tattoos were abundant in this crowd, and many of the guys displayed extensive body artistry on their arms, back, and neck. The South African men didn't follow the Anglo crowd and had varying amounts of hair on their heads, were clean-shaven, and to my surprise, not one sported a tattoo. Nobody wore earrings. Perhaps an employment condition banned ear jewelry. From this point on, I would never be out of sight of an Olive Security employee except for some after-work hours while safely in the confines of our contractor camp. There would always be a minimum of two Olive Security men in each armored vehicle, including the driver.

I watched as two Olive guys labored to raise the back lift-gate of this late model Chevy Suburban to stow my luggage. The weight of this armored vehicle was obvious, and I struggled to pull the heavy rear door shut as I climbed in the back seat. The manner in which this truck sat low to the ground and the very thick bulletproof windows all contributed to the appearance of it being a formidable vehicle to contend with.

Tinted windows and the dark body paint with the stubby little communication antennas made all the vehicles seem "official." Later confessions from the Olive guys revealed that these armored vehicles could withstand any small arms fire and maybe a poorly placed road bomb, but a rocket-propelled grenade (RPG) would penetrate us without question. It was a little unnerving to know our vulnerabilities.

As we made the transfer, four young children ran up to ask for food by looking up to the guards to establish eye contact, holding thumb and fingers together, and motioning to their mouths. If they got no response from one of the security men, they would go on to the next person, and on and on. These were cute children with dark complexions, broad smiles, and bare feet. Three were little girls ranging from six to eight years old; the fourth was a little boy, maybe about four or five years old. They spoke no English. I marveled at how tough their feet must be to traverse the hot and rough grounds of the surrounding areas. The gypsy-looking pullover dress each girl was wearing and the simple T-shirt and jeans the little boy wore gave them the appearance of average kids from the area. Little girls do not cover their heads in traditional Islamic fashion as adults do,

I would later find out. So, these girls showed their beautiful, long, brown hair with some natural curl, along with very simple jewelry of a necklace and bracelet. Each of them looked cared for and basically clean as far as children that play in such a dusty environment can be.

The security guys had a few bottles of water, oranges, and some other fruit and handed it all out to these kids. With waves for thanks, they graciously accepted the offerings and scurried off to a secluded corner of the lot to sit in the dust and divvy up. Eventually I learned that these children lived right next to the transfer point and were a familiar sight to our security teams making drops at that location. It was a bit shocking to me that they would run around unattended. *Where were Mom and Dad? Would I let my children run up to soldiers or any people with guns? And what about school? Were they well fed or in great need?*

As I learned more about the area and people, it became clear that most of the children I would see were not really begging, just average kids from the area hoping for some treat to be given to them by the Coalition forces. As the weeks went by during these first assignments in Iraq, I would discover much more about Iraqi children as I interacted with them a little and learned more about them through discussions with their parents.

We took off as a team of three vehicles from that talcum-powder-like dusty lot, driving up toward the buildings and through Safwan. Describing my first impression of Iraq is difficult. Dirty, impoverished, unkempt, squalid, backward, degraded? How come the difference? Why the stark contrast from the world I just left? How does an oil-rich country like

Iraq become this way? Trash littered the sides of the road, and potholes seemed to be commonplace in the streets. Two dead dogs lay off to the side of the road within a few hundred feet of each other. Flies were everywhere.

I could see businesses on the sides of the roads in small, primitive, adobe-mud buildings and tents. All these little shops and stores had hand-painted signs in Arabic on rough-cut sheet metal backgrounds fastened to some kind of scrap metal being used as a post or fence. It was crude, and I felt like I just stepped back in time.

The apparent family dwellings were square, single-level, tan, brick buildings with flat roofs. The bricks looked homemade and the layout work almost primitive. Junk metal was everywhere and adorned most every household's front yard. I was in shock at the difference from even the poorest town in the US I've ever been through. There was nothing to compare to. If one were to be blindfolded then released in Safwan Iraq and asked to guess where they were, I think the answer would be "Some third-world country in Africa."

Before getting onto the major highway and leaving Safwan we passed through one more interesting sight. The Olive guys called it "Main Street." I was looking at one of the largest outdoor markets in southern Iraq and could see junk vehicles for sale, scrap metal, empty drums, and abundant military surplus such as clothing and living supplies. A few crude tents were erected but most everything was out in the open. My Olive driver told me, "You can buy anything down there." I'm sure weapons and ammo were readily available; after all, wasn't military hardware the primary focus of the Saddam regime? It was becoming obvious that the government certainly didn't allocate proper funds on their people or infrastructure, at least not in this town. It all seemed kind of lawless and lacked structure.

Leaving the bumpy, pot-holed road of Safwan, you can go northerly toward Basra, or you can go east and a bit south to the seaport town of Umm Qasr, where an American base is located. A fairly new, interstate-style, blue traffic sign hung overhead with "Umm Qasr" in English and Arabic with a direction arrow. For us, the journey was northward toward Basra on the divided highway affectionately nicknamed Tampa. Since Central Command for Operation Iraqi Freedom is located at MacDill Airforce Base in Tampa, Florida, it didn't take much for me to make the connection.

Tampa was a smooth, modern, six-lane highway without potholes, constructed of black asphalt with faded, white, broken lines separating the lanes. We drove into sparse desert, flat and forbidding. Drifts of sand an inch or so deep covered the road every couple hundred yards. There was a substantial median between the northbound and southbound lanes, and we even passed a small "rest area"–style pull off on the right. A couple of broken cement tables and benches on a concrete pad sat in the open sun with a small swath of feeble trees in the background nearby. There must have been good days gone by when this might have been used by family travelers stopping for a break.

Iraq and the other Middle East countries drive on the right and use left-sided-steering vehicles. We passed several local vehicles that were mostly old, beat-up–looking, white-and-orange, 70s-vintage Toyota Land Cruisers and many small, older Datsun and Toyota mini pick-ups with a similar white color scheme. Again, a stark contrast to the Kuwait experience.

The Umm Qasr traffic sign was the last one I saw. But within a short distance after getting onto Tampa there was a large cement barricade off to the side of the road. It was spray painted with large, black-stenciled letters with the message to all in English: "Barrel Up, Slow Down, Respect Iraqis, and Other Road Users." I later noticed a few of these barriers strategically placed in the major thoroughfares reminding ourselves and our troops that courtesy is always top priority in this country.

The terrain was basically flat from horizon to horizon except for Sanam Mountain in the distance. The mountain rises high in the background and sits on the Kuwait-Iraq border. Its claim to fame is that it was the location of the surrender-signing event that ended Operation Desert Storm in 1991. Unfortunately, it has also been named as the location of an alleged massacre of many local citizens during Saddam's reign shortly after that surrender event.

In addition to the desert scrub brush that was so prevalent everywhere, sparse, little trees stood in scattered clumps on the horizon every so often. Off in the distance I could see an occasional lone tree reaching heights of twenty feet or more. Their pine tree appearance reminded me of a flowing, evergreen-type tree common to Florida and other tropical zones. I had to wonder about the marvels of nature and how plant life such as this didn't just dry up under day after day of beating heat.

Black smoke billowed from several scattered industrial facilities on the horizon. Overhead, black clouds formed from the continual release of burning waste gas. Open flames or "flares" could be easily seen from these smokestacks in bright daylight. A majority of the industrial sites in Iraq burn off their waste gas from oil wells, refineries, and other processes through these high smokestacks or even ground-level, open-flame pits. Legend has it that some of these flame pits have been burning since ancient times and that Daniel the prophet as well as Shadrach, Meshach, and Abednego were thrown into a furnace fueled by flames such as these.

As we made our way through the flat, open desert toward our camp at the Coalition base, I was surprised by the agricultural development and sheep herding that was within sight. I struggled to see any significant amounts of vegetation for these sheep to graze on, and I had to wonder about the heat. Somehow these sheep were immune to the hot desert temperatures. *Nature is marvelous*, I thought.

The housing we passed periodically seemed to be no more than mud-type structures with neatly arranged plats for small-scale gardening. A few larger structures had little flags flying over one corner of the building. These turned out to be the schools for children. No playground equipment or ball fields that I could distinguish, just primitive-looking houses that were a bit larger than the other buildings. Most of these little residential agricultural settlements had some sort of a well with a small, engine-driven pump arrangement visible from the road. I could see crude electrical lines supported on randomly placed, feeble poles feeding the majority of the dwellings. And of course, what would a mud dwelling be without a small satellite dish atop the roof?

Yes, despite the third-world atmosphere of this region, wherever I could see the overhead electrical lines reaching to each dwelling, chances were that there was a small satellite dish attached. Despite the out-of-place character of these gleaming reminders of modern society, they undoubtedly gave these homesteads a connection to the outside world from their remote location. But considering the overall condition of their dwellings, their vehicles, and their apparent meager resources, I would have expected media to be a lower priority. Maybe this was a Coalition program to get communication to the far reaches of the countryside? Perhaps these small farms had more money than was evident and the ouster of the dictatorship had cleared the way for purchase of these previously forbidden items.

As we continued on, we began to run into convoy traffic. Long, slow lines of privately- owned supply trucks, water tankers, and fuel tankers drove with an armored Humvee military vehicle at the lead and another at the tail. Helmeted soldiers manning machine guns kept their heads popped up as lookouts from these battle-worthy vehicles. Young children from the fields and houses would run up close to the road and stand there giving the thumbs-up to all military and convoy traffic that went past.

It was easy to distinguish us from local traffic. All of our vehicles were late model SUVs, and there were no late model vehicles driven by the locals. Every so often I would see adults working the fields nearby, as the children would scurry up to the road. Seems that Mom or Dad didn't discourage the children or forbid these roadside greetings but would just give a concerned glance and then resume their task at hand. I interpreted it as a nod of approval.

After traveling a short way on Tampa, we detoured around a damaged section of road, driving through sandy trails over oil pipelines. An insurgent attack on this pipeline had blown up the oil pipes that ran underneath the six-lane highway and basically melted the lanes above from the resulting fire. This incident happened just a few days before I arrived and made national news in the US and UK. There was concern from home about this also, so as any good husband would do, I left out the part about us driving directly through that section on the way to the base when communicating to loved ones back home that evening. Since convoy traffic with its lifeblood of water, fuel, and supplies into the country cannot afford to be disrupted, an alternate route for convoy trucks was established, but we still used the burnt highway detour that day.

We continued through the desert landscape on Tampa until we exited and proceeded onto the main road to the Coalition base. The road to the base was in good shape, allowing for high-speed travel. There were more dwellings and structures near the road on this stretch as well as more traffic. Small, crude stone shelters with scrap-metal-type roofs were set up as roadside businesses selling warm soda, local fresh fruits and vegetables, and other types of non-refrigerated goods. A fairly modern-looking cement factory was located off to one side, and scores of old, beat-up, well-worn dump trucks traversed up and down this main road.

A long line of run-down cars and trucks filled an apparent gasoline and diesel station to the point of causing a traffic jam, forcing us to drive around stopped vehicles. It was difficult to even tell it was a fuel station from looking at the bare, sign-less, beige brick building. There were only a few dingy, upright gas pumps in front, all underneath a corroded and weathered, hand-patched, metal awning supported on equally corroded and beat-up, round, metal columns. Junk vehicles, trash, and several scrap metal piles were strewn about the building perimeter itself.

The notion that Iraq would have gas lines never occurred to me, and the security guys were busy explaining many of these things to me as we drove on. But this road was also a dangerous section for insurgent activity since it was the main feed for the Coalition troops in the area. The litter and scrap metal piles, junked vehicles, dead animals, and other trash and debris would afford plenty of hiding places for roadside bombs. I decided the security men were telling me too much.

Soon we arrived at the entrance to Shaibah Logistic Base with our contractor compound located securely inside. This abandoned military base from the Saddam regime was now under Coalition control and run by the British. Several acres of junked military equipment littered the surrounding area as we approached the front. Not far from the entrance was an array of bright, white, two-room, metal office trailers lined up in neat rows on a gravel base. This would be home for over a hundred days on this trip. The compound itself was surrounded with an eight-foot, chain-link fence with barbed wire at the top, barbed wire rolls at the outside base, and a dark-colored vision obstruction webbing on the vertical runs of the fencing. Small bomb shelters erected above ground and fortified with sandbags were set up between every two trailers. Each shelter could hold about six to eight men.

Large water tanks on tall platforms were visible as we approached from outside the compound gate. Private guards from Nepal were on foot, toting automatic weapons and guarding the single-entry gate. They had a small, enclosed, air-conditioned guard shack just inside the entrance. These Nepalese men were referred to as Gurkhas by the UK nationals and are known for their loyalty and efficiency as soldiers.

Once inside the compound, two diesel generators roared away while we parked and unloaded gear. A room assignment was given to me, and I trudged through the gravel, dragging my belongings to my new home. The heat was utterly brutal, and I wanted to get out of the sun as soon as possible. Two bathrooms per trailer, the ever-so-important air conditioner in each room, some IKEA bedroom furniture and desk, satellite TV, and an internet connection would make the off-work hours more comfortable. I was whisked through a quick indoctrination, and I learned the basics about the camp.

The setup was acceptable. Laundry service was provided by local Iraqi men using washers and dryers set up in a dedicated trailer. Food was also done by locals in a military-style dining hall in the camp. An exercise room and recreation hall were available for all to use. Emergency medical facilities were available at camp, and the military base could take care of most any other needs. Since this was a civilian camp, alcohol was served after working hours at a bar run by one of the Olive guys as a volunteer position. Camp water could sometimes run out, and we were encouraged to be frugal while we showered. Cold, bottled water was available in refrigerated cases in the dining hall and recreation room, and each individual bedroom had a mid-size refrigerator for tenants to keep stuffed with water and any other goodies. It was stressed to me to drink plenty of water throughout the day.

In the early days of my time there, as I looked out on the open desert, the primitive buildings, and the harsh, ancient landscape, it really hit me that this is the land of Abraham. The ruins of Ur were not far from this very location. Joseph Smith's Jaredite interpreters originated from this part of the world. And now, at this point in history, there are probably a handful of Melchizedek Priesthood holders walking the very ground that Abraham walked on, myself included. That thought gave me goose bumps, and despite the fear and uncertainty of my future working in Iraq, I was thankful to be one of the few to have this privilege.

CHAPTER 5

It always seems that the interactions we have with people become some of the most fascinating aspects of our mortal life here on Earth. These interactions can also be a testing ground of our conduct, measuring how we apply the Savior's teachings in our lives. I was now in a realm of international cultures and values. Not just the Iraqi experience, which was about to begin, but a combination of British, Scottish, Welsh, Irish, Australian, Lebanese, Filipino, South African as well as Americans were all in the mix. On the individual level, it is usually self-interest that dominates the desire to participate in a project like this. But on the larger scale, it is always gratifying to see the ease with which diverse peoples can work in unity to accomplish a goal.

Being safely within the gates of the Coalition base, I began to meet those assigned to the project. As I started meeting the project staff, it became evident that this was an international mix of people, all men, and that working and living with these men would be an interesting experience. Brent was our site leader and an American. Pat was from Ireland and was working the electrical side of the project. Ikram was a Pakistani national and was working with instrumentation and controls. He was also a faithful, practicing Sunni Muslim, which became a useful bit of information to me later. Work had begun weeks earlier in July, and I replaced a French engineer who was not working well in the team environment. I was told there were some basic guidelines the Frenchman could not comply with. It was difficult for me not to speculate, and I surmised that the political climate at his home was not conducive for him to come to Iraq and render assistance. I learned later that his demeanor was arrogant and just plain obnoxious to the staff and local workers. Regardless, he wanted out, and I was willing to go in. Our international team was now going to incorporate me into the group.

We were performing a complete refurbishment of one of four natural gas–fired, combustion turbine and generator sets that supply power to the petrochemical facility where this machinery was located. Any excess power from these units was exported to the Ministry of Electricity, which is a fancy way of saying that it goes out to supply electricity to the local community. Complete refurbishment entailed removing the heavy casings that house the large, rotating, internal component, which is the power turbine rotor, and the power turbine rotor itself. Additionally, we would be removing the large, rotating generator core for some basic integrity checks and cleaning. Without knowing exactly what kind of conditions to expect, I anticipated some difficulty with tooling, equipment, and skilled labor. This work scope is a major project even in the most ideal conditions. All of the removed components would be replaced with rebuilt or new parts, and the machinery would be further assessed as disassembly took place.

Brent was a young, single, college-educated American and had been assigned there from the beginning of the contract by the parent corporation. He reported directly to the local representative of the US government agency with whom the contract was signed. A common practice in the industry, he was a corporate employee, whereas the majority of the older, more experienced professionals in this industry tended to be contract workers. Large corporations frequently assigned a younger employee with less experience to act as management to contract workers. This accomplished two important tasks: First, the less experienced could learn from the contractors any important details on the actual equipment rebuild procedures. This concept was akin to the Navy ensign right out of the academy being assigned to work closely with the well-seasoned chief petty officer. Second, young employees tended to be more submissive to corporate authority and could be a loyal source of feedback to upper management who have project responsibility at the corporate level. It would not be proper to portray contract employees as disloyal to their client. But when schedules, milestones, and logistical support of industrial projects did not meet expectations of the paying customer, a direct employee of the company was more likely to protect the interests and good name of his employer. As contractors, we tended to get quiet or give frank assessment when things out of our control did not execute as planned. This was especially true when the planning was done by those on the corporate side of the business, which was the more common practice.

Not long after being in the care of our security contractor and their teams, I began to realize they were top-notch.

State-of-the-art communications, late model armored vehicles, and GPS systems for tracking and route identification purposes were standard equipment. My first day out would be on a late-morning transport. The vehicles travel in groups of three or four, and our travel time to plant location would vary from forty to eighty minutes, depending on the chosen route for that day. By staggering departure times and routes, we would avoid setting travel patterns that could make us vulnerable.

The daily commutes to the plant and back were nerve-wracking, to say the least. Everyone wears a heavy piece of body armor, helmet, and safety glasses for personal protection. The roads were bumpy and pot holed. Often, there were long convoys of supply trucks causing us to travel slowly. Otherwise, our normal rate of speed in route was fast whenever possible. As fast as we could go was the rule and passing local traffic was standard procedure. It was common knowledge among the locals that almost any late model SUV was private security or a military team, and they would normally pull to the right and wave us on. When approaching an intersection, the lead vehicle in our team would pull out into the oncoming traffic lane and stop broadside, effectively blocking traffic while we entered the road and made our left or right turn. I saw the logic in this tactic, but I'm afraid it became a nuisance to some of the locals at times and possibly infuriated a few. It also made everyone aware of our presence in the area. Of course, there really was no hiding our identity as some form of military or Coalition officials. As we passed children working in the fields or walking to school, basically 100 percent of them would run up to the edge of the road and give the thumbs-up gesture to us. I would later learn from a good source that almost everyone in the local area knew we were there to help restore machinery and get power back on the grid. *That was great,* I thought, *not complete stealth as we would have preferred.* Local towns and nearby villages had combined populations in the hundreds of thousands, and getting the power back was essential for Iraq to build a more hopeful future.

We continued using bumpy, pot-holed back roads and convoy routes until the last few kilometers of the trip. Our final leg would be on the main road that passed by the petrochemical plant as it winds through the local towns. Our security team liked the road because it had multiple checkpoints, all manned by local police, with wide, flat, and clear shoulders on each side of the smooth, divided-lane highway. These local police checkpoints were a very primitive arrangement. Many were no more than two or three local policemen in uniform holding automatic weapons with no shelter and several pieces of broken, cement blocks or old tires set in the road to subject traffic to slow down. Sometimes there would be a worn-out sign propped up against a block of cement or an old tire with "Police Checkpoint – Slow Down" handwritten in black paint in Arabic and English.

Many times, we would approach these checkpoints to find the rather basic-looking policeman had been replaced with military, uniformed men, wearing full-face, black ski masks, or sometimes, the local, uniformed policemen would be there, wearing black ski masks themselves. The sight of those masked men can leave an indelible picture in one's mind and are a frightening sight. But the preparation and soothing calm of an experienced, private security contractor tiptoeing me through this scene for the first time kept me in check. These checkpoint guards would look us over quickly and give a go-ahead hand signal to each vehicle, allowing it to pass through. We would frequently comment that these men undoubtedly have the most dangerous job in Iraq.

There was only one way into our petrochemical facility and one way out. A large, billboard-sized picture of Imam Ali sits on the road after you turn into the facility. This historical figure was the Prophet Muhammad's cousin and son-in-law. After Muhammad's death in AD 632, there was a schism within the leadership of his followers. Ali claimed he was entitled to be successor by virtue of his kinship to Muhammad, while a ruling oligarchy decided that Abu Bakr would be the leader. This is the origin of the Shia Muslims and Sunni Muslims. Followers of Ali became Shia or Shiites as we know them today. They predominate in Iran, Iraq, and various pockets throughout the Middle East. As I got to know the Iraqi labor and management over the course of our project, I was surprised to learn who the Sunni Muslims were amongst the mostly Shiite staff and workers. The bitter animosity that I had been led to believe existed between Shiite and Sunni Muslims was just nowhere to be found. Actually, it was quite the contrary.

As we approached the front gate to the plant, a final checkpoint manned by plant personnel with automatic weapons required some vehicle maneuvering around makeshift barriers, and then the hand signal clearance to pass through was given.

The final few hundred feet before actually passing through the gate into the plant was a busy scene. There were beat-up taxis and old buses with clouds of black diesel soot smoking from their clanking engines. Plenty of old, well-worn cars were everywhere. All this vehicle activity was engaged in dropping off workers. Vendors lined up on the sides, selling produce and dried goods from crudely fabricated handcarts or primitive shelters erected with scrap metal for roofing with mud brick walls. It was semi-chaotic. We would zip through this scene many times to come. I soon discovered that there were several thousand people employed at this plant, and everyone came through the same front gate. A portion of the employees lived within the facility boundaries, but I never could find out how many were housed there.

The inside of the plant was typical of what the surrounding countryside was like in terms of general neglect and disrepair. Broken vehicles lay about. Hunks of steel frames and carcasses of machine components were piled next to buildings and the warehouse. Plenty of trash stowed up in windswept corners of buildings and storm drain culverts. The front administration building appeared to have been neatly landscaped in years gone by with several native species of trees and some small bushes. It was a four-story, orange-colored, stone building with a worn and weathered painted sign in English and Arabic displaying the government ownership of this facility. As we pushed through the main route around the side of the administration building and toward our power plant section, large groups of men walking to their workplace would stop, turn, and stare.

For the first few trips into the plant, this was an intimidating event to me. I didn't feel particularly threatened, but nonetheless, there were many of them and few of us. Since the job had been ongoing since mid-summer, this stop-and-look ritual was a normal and daily occurrence. Getting nervous, apprehensive, or intimidated wasn't necessary, but it's still a basic, human reaction. After all, we were from the occupying force, and we had an armed escort with us. It wasn't long into the job when I discovered a way to break that ice successfully. Additionally, as time passed, I realized that many times our security team drivers were overzealous with their driving patterns after entering the plant. Some of the security men were just recently rotated from Baghdad projects and had a "Go! Go! Go!" mentality. So, when the armored vehicles came roaring through the plant, there was good reason for pedestrians to take notice and be cautious.

The power plant section and our office trailer were a short way through the plant from the main entrance gate and the administration building. For the environment we were in, our modern, air-conditioned office trailer was somewhat out of place with the dilapidated surroundings. We were still on a main thoroughfare for vehicle traffic and foot travel to deeper sections of the facility. First order of business when arriving was to allow the security team to check the immediate work area for any type of bombs or tampering while we waited in the vehicles. There was trash, some new portable toilets, old oil barrels, and several, forty-foot-long, steel storage containers in the vicinity of the office trailer. Several straggly looking dingo-type dogs were sniffing through the trash and took off for cover when the guards got out of the vehicles.

Quick checks finished, and it was out of the vehicles we would go, body armor removed and gear and laptops retrieved from the vehicle rear storage. We had a portable satellite that gave us internet connectivity to the corporate systems necessary for access to technical documentation and email communications. The inside of the trailer was fully open with several desks against the walls, a server with internet hookups, several large, metal file cabinets, and a small refrigerator. Everyone would come in and set up their laptops to check their connections, then head out to the machinery to check work progress. Since this was my first day, I would get "the tour" and be introduced to the Iraqi management and labor force working with us.

Just a few yards across the road from the trailer was the rear entrance to the power plant building. A few of the plant workers were walking past as we crossed the road heading into the building. All of these men were dressed in nice, clean, Western-style clothing, which was usually a long-sleeved, collared shirt without a tie and nice slacks with street shoes or sandals. We got the usual attention from them with everyone looking at us. So, I took a little initiative, smiled, and kind of nodded my head in one of those "Hello, how'ya doing" type gestures. One or two of the group sort of nodded back in return, then they all turned their heads forward while they continued walking. It might be the armed guards that accompanied us wherever we went in the plant that caused the intrigue, but we certainly were the center of attention. Most likely it had been awhile since Westerners were in the plant in any capacity, and our presence there was still a curiosity to everyone.

Many of our private security guards were an oddity, even by Western standards. The majority of them were from the UK and Caucasian, with shaved heads or close-cropped hair and arms usually loaded with tattoos. Since I was the new guy that day, the plant workers were probably just checking me out and not staring at the guards. As I became more accustomed to our private security guards, I noticed a distinct difference in behavior depending upon nationality. This would become interesting in the future.

The power plant building itself was a light-colored, faded steel structure about two stories tall and seemed to be in pretty good condition. Some Arabic graffiti adorned the lower reaches in one section close to the rear entrance. Otherwise, it looked like fresh paint had not been applied to the building exterior for many years, if at all. Walking out onto the main floor of the power plant, I looked at a sight, that was by this time, somewhat expected. There were four 1970s-vintage gas turbines in two rows within the enclosed building. But it was the condition of the machinery and the surrounding area that was unusual. One of the turbines was serviceable, while the other three were in pieces. The roofs to the equipment enclosures of the three out-of-service units were removed and stacked up upon each other. The large casings and internal rotating assemblies were removed and not within sight. Paint was chipped or gone entirely from the exterior sections, and large, rusty, corroded patches were everywhere. I could see where smaller components had been removed and most likely used elsewhere. There were many plates, fittings, and piping sections that were obviously handmade. Dirt, oil, water, and trash could be found in many different areas that would be expected to be clean and dry due to electrical cable routing. Many pieces of the cannibalized machinery lay in walkways, haphazardly placed in piles without any protection from the elements or other damage. I have never been to a turbine junkyard (nor do I believe that such a place exists), but this could be a glimpse of what it would look like. It was obvious that the plant staff had scavenged these units sometime in the past to keep units elsewhere running.

There was still the running unit. It was loud and required hearing protection if you wanted to walk up to it and look. The plant maintenance crew had constructed small troughs and gutters to catch oil leaks from offending areas of the machine. Smoke spewed out of several of the hot compartments. All of the compartment doors were open to assist in ventilating the machinery. It was apparent that the factory-designed ventilation scheme was out of service with broken fans, cut wires, and removed ventilation ducts. Our young site leader, Brent, accompanied me, and I asked how much output this unit was getting at this time. He said about one-half of normal. That was the best it could perform. I noticed plant personnel working and walking near the unit without any hearing protection. For me, I couldn't stand the noise, and it physically hurt. At the minimum, I would have to plug my ears with my fingers as I walked by.

As we approached the end of the power building, I passed close to the workshop where some of the plant workers would leave their gear, eat their lunch, and take breaks and mingle. A large group of them happened to be congregated off in the back, and we all made eye contact. They were consistent in their appearance. Clean shaven with a neatly trimmed haircut and moustache seemed to be the prevailing grooming standard. Everyone in the group wore blue work overalls, with one of them also wearing traditional Arab headgear. The quick glance I took of their footwear showed it wasn't up to safety standards, and I worried about this much more in the weeks to come. The noise was still deafening at this point, and I still had my fingers in my ears. I dropped my hands but lifted my right hand about to shoulder height as a "Hello" and gave a smile. We were walking swiftly at this point to exit the building and heading toward the power plant control room. As we exited, I caught a glimpse of return waves with right hands in the air and smiles from my soon to be work companions. It occurred to me to just be nice, wave, and acknowledge people as we crossed paths. Without planning it, I had stumbled upon a customary greeting that became my trademark.

Going on toward the control room, I got to practice my greeting again on a few groups of men and received return greetings successfully. It seemed that I had possibly found a way to break the ice, and it made me feel better. So many times at home and other places familiar to us, we tend to go about our business without regard for others that we pass by. Maybe it's the sheer volume of people that makes us withdraw into a bubble, where we execute our agenda and turn a blind eye to those around us. Not that we see strangers as "in the way," but we tend to focus on ourselves and become oblivious to those around us. I was grateful to be able to acknowledge these people with a wave and a smile. Without knowing many of the details of this society's struggles at this point, I felt sincerity and humbleness in their return greetings to me, especially since I was a visitor in their land. The first three verses of Hebrews chapter 13 stood out in my mind after this experience, and I found it fulfilling to comply with that scriptural counsel from the apostle Paul: "Let brotherly love continue. Be not forgetful to entertain strangers: for thereby some have entertained angels unawares. Remember them that are in bonds, as bound with them; and them which suffer adversity, as being yourselves also in the body."

After quickly skirting through the work areas and into the control room, we passed through a broken metal door where I saw a somewhat familiar sight. Many of the control room operators sat around one well-worn, metal worktable in the middle of the room with maybe five or six equally well-worn, metal chairs. A couple of men stood or talked, and a few watched instrumentation gauges on the large monitoring panels built into the walls. All of the men were dressed well in Western-style shirts and slacks and seemed to be attentive to the conversations they were engaged in. This is typical for a control room atmosphere except the lighting was dim, the walls yellowed, and the design of the indicators and monitoring panels were definitely out of date and looked every day of their almost thirty years. Even the worktable and chairs seemed to be the correct décor for this environment. A quick smile and wave and then return greetings were given from all those watching us.

Our destination was the plant management offices where I'd be formally introduced to the plant engineers and plant manager of the power plant section. A walk down a dingy, dark hallway passing several offices on the right and we were there. All of the office doors looked original: a metal, commercial-style door with the upper half a large frame of glass that allowed a clear view into each office. It didn't appear that there was any new office furniture in the rooms that I looked into. Old window-unit air conditioners hung in each office, and they also looked like the originally installed units or possibly replacement units that had been installed a very long time ago. There were a few women walking past in traditional Islamic dress with full headscarves and open faces. They avoided eye contact as we passed by. Everything kind of reminded me of an old 1960s school building with worn and broken entrance doors and dim lighting.

I met Malik, the plant manager. He looked like the typical Iraqi man in his early forties, but he was taller than most Iraqis. We could talk eye to eye since both of us were just above six feet tall. A well-groomed mustache and neatly trimmed hairstyle rounded out his slim physique with lightly graying hair color and dark-olive complexion. His English sounded excellent, and we greeted each other with firm handshakes. Malik summoned for the rest of his staff to come for introductions, and soon I was surrounded by eight to ten men shaking my hand and speaking some kind of greeting in Arabic and some broken English. Everyone was enthusiastic and smiling. I made a comment at this time to all of them that they must be the big brains behind the operation of the plant and that I was glad to meet them. Unknown to me, this statement got caught up in a mistranslation which I'd have a chance to work out later.

Malik and I got off to a good start. Eventually, we would have some very spiritual conversations, and I would get opportunities to explain gospel principles to him as he would explain Islamic principles to me. Since Brent was a young, single man, I think Malik and I had more of a kinship. We were both married men with young children still at home. There was mutual interest in cultural differences that both of us were anxious to inquire about. For the time being, he was concerned that we were comfortable while at the plant and that all the proper documentation was available to us for our work.

I couldn't help but feel we were imposing on these people to some extent. There we were in his office with armed guards holding AK-47s outside in the hallway as we went through introductions and business discussions inside. But there was a difference in this scenario. Our security guards were there for our protection. There was no pressure or mandate for plant personnel to cooperate or comply with our directions. Actually, Malik and his staff and all the plant workers had developed a unique relationship with our security guards. They would always greet each other and ask how they were doing. I would learn that soda, food, and local fruits were constantly being traded and given away between the plant workers and our security guards as well as ourselves. When rotations would come and guards would leave for other locations, heartfelt goodbyes were always traded between the plant workers and guards before anyone's departure. Many times, the plant workers would approach us to inquire about health and happiness of previously assigned security guards. Despite the sometimes-stark contrast of our guards physical appearance and the plant workers, there was a friendly atmosphere between the two groups.

We concluded that visit and were invited back for lunch in a few hours. The standard routine for our noon meal was a sack lunch provided by the contractor camp dining facility. Two unappealing sandwiches, some fresh veggies such as carrots and cucumber slices, a small bag of potato chips from Kuwait, and a warm can of Coke or Sprite was the daily ration to sustain life during the workday. Being new on the job, I hadn't had grown sick of the midday fare at this point and didn't realize what a treat was in store for us. We parted company with Malik for a while to look at machinery, parts, and tooling located at the turbine deck and near the mechanic's workshop area. I quickly got up to speed on the work scope, the available tools, and the plant labor assigned to work on the machinery with us.

Back to the workshop area and several of the mechanics filtered in. I met them all one by one. It was tough trying to remember their names. As I struggled a bit with pronunciations, someone started passing around a magic marker and the men started writing an English version of their name on the front of their hard hat for my benefit. Several of them could speak a couple English words and practiced on me. Everyone was shuffling around, so putting a name to a face was impossible to me at this time. Writing names on the hard hats was a welcomed gesture. It was getting near lunchtime, so we concluded our meetings and assessments and headed back over to Malik's office for lunch.

Malik and the other men had just concluded saying their noonday prayers and were busy preparing for our lunch gathering. It was a classic lunch. A large, ornate mat was spread out on the office floor with enough room for about a dozen of us to sit cross-legged on the floor in a circle. The mat was the same style as those used to say noonday prayers, but they added a plastic cover over the center to contain food spills. These were beautifully stitched patterns that we might see in the US sold as Persian carpets or rugs. Even the simplest patterns of these mats that I've seen since that day were all elegant constructions with a cotton or wool fabric. Everyone removed their shoes as per custom and sat knee to knee on the outer area of the mat.

The center was filled with a large assortment of homemade food in well-used aluminum and ceramic bowls evenly spread out. Everyone had warmed the food, although I noticed that there were no microwave ovens in sight. Seems that hotplates are the prevalent method of food warming before meals. I believe that availability of microwaves in Iraq is not as much an issue anymore as it is the cost of a microwave oven being prohibitive for an individual's income or maybe the facility's budget. Nevertheless, a cornucopia of local food was displayed, hot and available to dig in. There was no grace or opening prayer as I expected, just a polite restraint until all were seated and ready to pass the bowls of food around. Plates were not used. Instead, full pieces of round, pita-type bread were passed out to everyone and were used similar to a plate. Spoons were distributed. If you saw something you liked that was out of reach, then a polite passing of that bowl would come your way and you were expected to scoop a few spoonfuls onto your pita bread plate and pass the bowl back.

It was a great feeling to have all the attention of our gracious hosts while we sampled the many foods. Everyone wanted us to try this and try that. It felt similar to a flock of proud grandmothers wanting to stuff their grandchildren with all their favorite goodies at a family gathering. Dishes that consisted of rice topped with baked and peeled-and-cut potatoes with a chicken-based broth were common. Fried fish in olive oil, cubed beef in a dark broth mixed with cut potatoes then spooned over rice, and a soon-to-be favorite of mine, *Sambousik*, were all available in abundance. The *Sambousik* were small, triangular pies filled with ground beef, usually paired with peas and slices of carrots with some nuts, and wrapped in a thin, flour-based pastry dough that was fried in olive oil. The spice in the meat seemed to be some kind of nutmeg or other sweet spice that complemented this delectable morsel. There didn't seem to be any curry-based dishes as I would have expected. As the passing of bowls and sampling of dishes subsided, everyone ended up with one or two main courses within arm's reach and would begin eating straight out of the bowls with their spoons. Maybe two or three of us would be sharing a bowl. If you wanted to get a little taste of another dish that you missed, you just reached over and spooned out a big scoop or two and put it in the bowl you were sharing with your "table mates" or onto the pita bread plate. Many of the men would spoon their medley right onto bite-sized pieces of their pita bread and roll it all up as a single-bite serving. There were no piles of napkins or paper towels put out.

Conversation died down after a while, and the focus turned to us, the two Americans, Ikram, our Pakistani instrument engineer, and Pat, the Irish electrical engineer. Malik said to me that there was some confusion in my comment about being pleased to meet the "big brains" behind the plant operations. It was totally quiet now with all eyes on me, and I saw the interpretation mix-up. They took the meaning as "big head" or proud and arrogant. So, I replied "No, no, that's not possible, none of you are French!" There was no translation needed—the entire room roared in laughter. They knew my original comment's intent now. It was made clear to me beforehand that there would be a good bit of damage recovery operations for me to do with the plant workers to get the work momentum going forward. Maybe a little humor with this small shot at the man I was replacing was a start.

It was unfortunate that this is the impression the French national left with these people. As I grew more accustomed to the nationalities of the men that would work with us, I noticed a distinct difference in conduct, thought, and humility, depending on national origin. My Iraqi hosts were warm, kind, and considerate. And, in this instance, they displayed their acceptance of our team by inviting us into their culture for a noon meal. Later, I learned how exceptionally forgiving our Iraqi hosts actually were. They excused the Frenchman long ago, citing his probable personal problems or even his health. Sadly, Americans have their traits too. Whether these are perceptions based on Western media or local media, I never really found out. But I would have to deal with several of these preconceptions eventually.

At the conclusion of our meal, some rough paper towels were passed out, we cleaned up, and all shook hands again as a thank you and goodbye for the time being. It was a wonderful experience for me. I noticed the others in our team were ready to get back to work, except Ikram and myself. We were both enjoying the social gathering, and Ikram was using some of his Arabic skills. To me, there is nothing better than connecting with people, and our hosts demonstrated a fine example of socialization during their daily lunch break. The entire episode was similar to a family gathering with lots of talking, laughing, and sharing with one another. This was a male-only function, but after spending time with my hosts and getting to know their character, I am confident that all their conversation at that lunch were clean and upright in nature.

Despite what any of these men may have been through in the past, they still appeared to be pure of heart, humble, and grateful to Heavenly Father for their blessings. In our case, they were gracious and accepting of others. My experience in America has been when a group of men gather together for a meal, the conversation drifts into lewd jokes and sexual discussion. What a welcome breath of air to be in the company of these men. I could feel their spirit of gratitude and their bond as workers and friends. Just as the scriptures tell us that adversity humbles us and brings us closer to God, a side effect must be that it brings us closer to one another. Any of us that have gone through the death of a loved one, a painful divorce, or a debilitating illness realize the value of friends and family. I cannot help but think that the years of poverty, oppression, and tragedy have cemented a binding force among these people that extends far beyond their professional affiliations. How rich they are to have this strong kinship among themselves similar to our ward family relationships but on a professional level as well as a social level.

During my time at BYU, I felt this kinship to a certain degree while doing a co-op assignment at Geneva Steel. While we didn't pray together as the Iraqis do, there was still a bond that tied us together, which kept us helping each other to work together and accomplish our tasks. That particular Utah experience was distant in my memory until my first day on the job in Iraq. Without yet getting to know the rest of the men I would be working with on the plant floor, I was confident that their character would be in harmony with their management team. As the days went by and names and personalities of the workforce began to take root with me, I was not disappointed.

Having now been in Iraq for no more than forty-eight hours, I was getting a piece of the big picture. The phrase "rebuild effort" lacks the depth of meaning that the undertaking is. There is a human side to this task: rebuilding lives. Many of us might believe that due to American bombs and missiles, we are obligated to repair what we damaged. While this is true for specific locations, Iraq as a whole has suffered significantly from corruption, neglect, international isolation, and the ineptitude of a despotic regime. The natural wealth of the country could have easily supported the basic infrastructure of its industrial backbone. This facility itself could have been a self-supporting, industrial plant that could have provided employment, a

marketable product, and revenues for upkeep and modernization as the years went by. Instead of living up to its potential,
the facility was stifled and incapable due to the condition of its
equipment, the lack of upgrades and modernization, and the
omission of competing in the modern global economy.

It's likely many of us have felt that when we don't live up
to our potential, we can become discouraged and depressed.
As my time in Iraq progressed beyond these first impressions, I
watched carefully but didn't see discouragement and depression
as widespread. On the contrary, I saw hope, promise, and smiling faces. The parable of the talents teaches the principle that
we should enlarge what we are given. Maybe in the Western
societies we take this principle literally, and this is where some
of the fullness of life can be missed. We take the talents and try
to improve and enlarge them by excelling in our professional
life, our societal status, and even our church callings. If we have
tried fervently to be the perfect teacher or leader, do we miss
some needed interaction with those around us? It seems to me
that we can easily become engaged in business and accomplishment, and that it can become secondary to concern ourselves
with living souls. My Iraqi hosts did not have this pressure to
achieve and accomplish. It didn't matter that these were the
plant engineers, and they were at the top of the professional
level. There was a definite distinction of roles and hierarchy in
relation to their duties and responsibilities, but they had refined
their relationships to each other and their subordinates with
respect, courtesy, and brotherly love. I feel they took their talents and built them in the direction they could—that direction

being the human relation with each other and their conduct with people.

After the first day and the introductions, we began to settle into a routine. Evenings in the camp were interesting due to the international mix of security and engineers involved in the local projects. Several cell and satellite phones were available for our use to talk to loved ones back home when signal strength was good. Many of us would band together to take an evening walk and engage in conversation dealing with family, politics, current events, and work issues. Of course, the verbiage would drift into forbidden areas where I would opt out, absorb the teasing, insults, and insinuations, and try to be a good example. Actually, as time passed, the conversations tended to stay on the clean side whenever I was in the group. This is not really any kind of phenomenon, but sort of a natural evolution of self-guilt and maybe some lone peer pressure. As long as I held to my values, refusing to participate or just plain ignoring the "gutter" talk, people tended to develop respect and accommodate me. When holding to high standards, I believe we affect those around us for the positive. Too often we feel threatened by the negative, and we fear its influence on us. While this is a major concern that parents struggle with in regard to their children, how easy it is to forget that the world is fertile ground for the wheat as well as the tares. By holding to the iron rod in public forums outside of our ward and family settings, we are being "the salt of the earth" and are engaged in missionary work by example alone. This is always a goal of parents: to have children choose the right when in the presence of the wrong. It's also the eternal plan for us, to be tested on a day-to-day basis, which in turn will provide us with experience that should strengthen us in our eternal progression.

It was strange to see the contrast of culture between the Iraqi workers during the day at the plant and my Western colleagues in the evenings back in the camp. After sharing some basic gospel principles and the First Vision during some of the evening walks, I met the usual resistance, but I was still surprised to discover that even today how little is known about the LDS faith and history outside of the American continent. One Scottish colleague questioned everything I would say and finally took some offense. He summed it all up in his mind and would tell me in a teasing, sarcastic tone, "Well, then it's God bless America . . . and nobody else."

Ikram, our Pakistani engineer, took a different approach and was curious about my strict values. He was a committed Sunni Muslim, and we both noticed there were many lifestyle similarities between us. Eventually he accepted a Book of Mormon in English and appreciated that I would offer it to him. We became good friends and spent many hours discussing cultural, political, and religious topics between ourselves in the evenings at camp. During the workday, I likewise conversed with the Iraqi men and enlisted Ikram's help clarifying any Islamic principles as they were explained to me by the Iraqi men. All in all, it was a whirlwind of cultural extremes on a day-to-day basis.

CHAPTER 6

In late summer in southern Iraq, evenings and mornings didn't differ much. It was still hot but bearable. But the midday heat was so brutal, the motivation to conduct business or perform manual labor was zapped right out of me. Dry heat still causes sweating, and water became my best friend. I lost my appetite during the hot hours and focused on keeping hydrated and looking for ways to get out of the sun while walking between work areas. Dry heat temperatures above 120°F for days in a row were not uncommon. Day after day of cloudless skies and beating sun throughout September and October were the norm. Sunglasses were essential to keep the snow blindness to a minimum during the midday hours. The evening hours confirmed the harsh character of the land with the open flames on the horizon reaching upward and lighting up the night sky. It was always difficult to see many stars. The ever-present talcum powder–like dust was everywhere and penetrated everything. With this fine abrasive clinging to everything that takes up space, it's no wonder that machinery and equipment subject to this environment have high failure rates and a rapid decline of performance.

The facility mechanical and electrical workers arrived every morning around 7:30 a.m. in a well-worn, 1970s-vintage metropolitan bus from the local population centers a distance away from the plant. A typical work week in Iraq is a six-day schedule, with Friday taken off as the Sabbath day throughout the Islamic world. The workdays are shorter, and everyone leaves by about 2 p.m. Of the twenty-odd men that I got to know eventually, I learned only four or five of them owned a vehicle of any kind. They couldn't afford one, and their financial priorities focused on family living requirements. The men dressed similar for the commute to and from work. Nice slacks, a long- or short-sleeved, casual dress shirt tucked in, and dress shoes or a fancy style of leather sandals. Only a few of the bus occupants wore traditional Arab garb and headgear. Everyone was well groomed and used an after shave or fragrant deodorant that could be clearly noticed, especially in the hot, dusty environment. For the plant staff that I saw, there were no gruff-looking or unkempt individuals. The women had the same high standard of dress. Mostly solid-pattern, long dresses that reached the ankles, with long-sleeved tops of a variety of conservative patterns. Nothing fancy, sharp, or extravagant. All the women wore simple head-scarves of various dark-colored patterns, the goal being to cover the hair completely. The predominate footwear for the women seemed to be sandals or other types of open-toed high heels that strap above the ankle. I watched all the locals defy the heat and dress modestly and conservatively. It seemed to me their clothes were a demonstration of self-respect and dignity with their positions in the workplace and their status in society.

I kept up my new custom of smiling and briefly waving to those whose path I crossed throughout the workday. Smiles and return waves were standard by now. It seemed to relieve some tension, if not for them, then for myself. My colleagues never really grasped this concept, but they were still polite and cordial in their greetings and conversations with the workforce. A firm handshake to the guys in the morning with my usual "Hello" or "Good morning" was my plan, in order to learn their names and begin to assess their abilities. It became evident that they were just as anxious to teach me some Arabic language skills and introduce me to local customs as I was to teach them industrial skills. So, the importance of the morning greeting was an underestimated factor in my plan to get to know the men. In their culture, this morning contact is very important to them. They don't just walk in and give off a grumbled "Good morning," then retreat to their workspaces; they greet and socialize. The culture promotes this socializing, and the bond between them was plain to see. Soon they'd taught me the Arabic greeting in the region. "Salaam Alikum" is said first by the person who offers the greeting. The recipient then replies with "Alikum Salaam." Roughly translated, the greeter says, "Peace (God) be with you," and the response is, "And God be with you." The men got a total charge out of this interaction. I think they kind of adopted me into their circle at that point, and within the next day, I was taught the full sequence of the local greeting custom of the region. A firm handshake is given while saying "Salaam Alikum," and then, with hands still gripped, each man pulls right shoulder into right shoulder for a gentle bump and sometimes a pat on the back with the left hand. Additionally, I was determined to learn some basic Arabic words that would help us communicate in the workplace.

My routine to greet the workers in their workshop area every morning paid off. We learned much about each other in short order. It was easy to let our personalities go their natural course, and everyone was being themselves within just a few days. There was no apprehension, only complete acceptance. A total of twelve men in the mechanic crew would be working side by side with me for the next three and a half months. Despite the language barrier, I learned many things about them, and they learned many things about me. About half of them had a vocabulary of a few basic English words. There were another ten to twelve men from the other work crews that I had daily interaction with throughout the project, and they had about the same level of English vocabulary. Most of their English skills were recently acquired and many of the words were learned from British and American TV shows and movies played on Arabic satellite networks using subtitles. Several of them had home computers with a Windows 98 or Millennium operating system that had only English language installed. Computers are expensive relative to income in Iraq, but they are now starting to flourish since the regime was overthrown. The men explained that satellite TV and use of English had been forbidden during the Saddam years. In spite of the language barrier, we did okay with the communication as a whole, especially as we got more comfortable as a team and developed special communication skills with our limited vocabulary. I became a master at pantomime, throwing in the few Arabic words I'd learned with English terms they were likely to know and getting the message across with plenty of snickers, smiles, and laughter from the men. We were not supplied a translator as I had hoped.

I quickly realized that as soon as I used English in conversation with any of the men, it was crucial for me to be thinking of an alternate way to say the same thing. This amounted to a continual thesaurus churning in my head. Several times I would remind my English-speaking colleagues to say the same thing in a different way if they got a blank stare from their workers. Saying the same phrase slower and louder was not the preferred method and could be insulting. It was embarrassing at times to see this take place, so I would often jump in and try to clarify. As a visitor in any foreign land, it is courteous to acknowledge local customs and to rid ourselves of the notion that we should be accommodated. Maybe the novel *The Ugly American* should be standard reading for Westerners before working in Iraq, or elsewhere, for that matter. It was the objective of the workers and me to work together to accomplish our task using the resources available. Many times, my Iraqi workers would demonstrate how resourceful they could be using the available skills, knowledge, or tooling at their disposal.

The plant engineer that worked closely with me to help with mechanical assembly was a young man named Mohammad. He'd been educated locally in Iraq in their university system, was married with two small children, and had a good vocabulary of English. Not as large as Malik and about ten years younger, Mohammad was an anxious learner and had the respect of the ten plant mechanics he had authority over. Actually, most of the men were thin and smaller in stature than I expected. The majority of the pictures I have from that time have me leaning over a bit so I wouldn't feel like I was towering over them.

It only took a few days to realize that because Mohammad was younger, sometimes the mechanics would take turns poking a little fun at him. We found the common English word "baby" was one that all of us understood. The guys wanted me to know that they realized Mohammad was young for this position. Eventually the men would coax me to go along with some teasing, and I would agree with them out loud and say in the form of a question "Mohammad-baby?" while turning full circle, looking for Mohammad. The phrase was taken as "Mohammad, you're too young for this job (you are still a baby)!" He would smile back, bark at them in Arabic, and tell me in English that they were just jealous. He knew the men put me up to this and jokingly scolded them for enticing my participation. Mohammad always referred to the men as "the guys" when talking to me, and the phrase stuck. I noticed that there were never any intense moments or major arguments among the guys. Genuine debate over a procedure or validation of a completed task came up every now and then. But Mohammad had a great relationship with his workers. Ironically, most of the crew were around Mohammad's age. Maybe they really were a little jealous.

Over time I was able to communicate to the guys some of my core values of the Latter-day Saint lifestyle. A couple of the guys smoked the prevailing brand of local cigarettes, and I would let them know it was bad for them and that they should quit. After they taught me the word "moo-raa-ha," which means "no good," I would shake my finger at them when they would light up and say, "Moo-raa-ha," and then pantomime that I was choking to death and start coughing. The other workers would chime in with smiling faces, backing me up with verbal Arabic snippets of some kind telling their coworkers I was right. Whenever any of the smokers had a task to do, I would pretend that it took them extra time to do the task. I would stand nearby with one hand on my hip, tapping a foot, raising my wristwatch to my face up and down a couple times, and mimicking them smoking a cigarette. It was a humorous way to get after them for smoking those things. The other guys would jump in on the fun and before long everyone, including the other smokers, would be yelling in Arabic that it was taking too long and that they should stop smoking those rotten cigarettes. All the guys knew that I was espousing a value to them in a friendly way, and nobody took offense.

The term "*Ali-Baba*" was common ground also. Whenever I couldn't find a tool, my flashlight, or something else, all the guys would start looking around accusing each other of being Ali-Baba, while several of them scurried around looking for my lost item. Ali-Baba is a connotation for thief the same way Benedict Arnold connotes a traitor to us. We had developed a relationship. It was evident that laughter and smiles were going to be a part of our communication tools, so we would try to have fun throughout the workday.

Mohammad was interested in my peculiar lifestyle compared to the stereotypical American man. As the guys worked on the equipment, I stood close by to watch and direct as needed. We initiated small talk when the better English speakers were there. I openly lamented one day that I couldn't see any local sites in Iraq due to the danger and security. I had expressed my desire to go to Ur, which was some distance away but within range of a day's trip. Mohammad informed me he was from there, and everyone was caught off guard and couldn't understand why I would even know of Ur. When I explained that I wanted to see the birthplace of Abraham, I guess it took everyone by surprise. They were intrigued that I even knew of the birthplace of Abraham. Most likely this was a motive they never thought they would see from an American. It was probably an oddity to them to meet a middle-aged American that was happily married, didn't approve of infidelity or premarital sex, and was a non-drinker and non-smoker. Many times, the guys would quiz me to see if I had drunk alcohol the night before. They knew the character of Bruce and some of our security guards and assumed that I was free to do as I pleased too. They quizzed me on fidelity issues, asking about "soldier girls" on the base. I would just point to my wedding ring, then shake my head no. They would all smile and confirm among themselves what I meant. But trying to explain to them that I was free to do as I pleased, yet I chose to obey the commandments was a difficult task.

What I quickly learned was that just as we can be led to perceive that many Muslims are violent or vengeful, they tend to perceive that many Westerners are hedonistic and selfish. And can we blame them? What does our media demonstrate to them as we blare out sex-joke-saturated sitcoms, lewd movies, and reality shows that glorify deceit and selfishness? All this is produced by our society for the world to see and then form an opinion of us. With issues such as gay marriage, divorce rates, and agnosticism, how else would we be perceived by those of a theistic and austere culture? They probably see us as the images described in the eighth chapter of Mormon that alludes to a culture glorifying materialism and promoting self-indulgence. While even the Christian religious institutions of our time show evidence of decadence and complacency, we know that this is not the state of our entire society. But the perception is there and the bad overshadows the good and affects the view from afar. Just as in Iraq, the bad news of bombings, killings, and evil acts against its citizens overtakes the good news of liberty, economic growth, the overall goodness of the people, and the rebuilding of lives that is taking place.

The men and I were off to a good start, and we soon discovered we shared many values between our two lifestyles: no profanity, alcohol, lewd discussion; respect and reverence toward each other; and gratitude to God for life and family. I decided to learn more Arabic words and make my stance known on my values whenever the situation would arise. I naturally drifted toward the better English speakers at first, so I engaged in as much dialogue as possible with them. One of the better English speakers was our tool room attendant, Galib, and we got to be very conversational together on a daily basis. Galib was from Hilla, which is near Baghdad and close to Babylon. He was in his mid-fifties, was thin and taller than a lot of the guys and smoked too much. After we had known each other awhile, I was not shy about chastising him over his smoking, and he took it as genuine concern and not any kind of self-righteous behavior on my part. He had worked at the facility since its construction by a Western company in the mid-seventies and moonlighted on weekends as a tour guide at Babylon. This is where he developed his English skills, and he was more than happy to have someone to practice with. Eventually he would teach me the local greeting from Hilla, which placed cheek to cheek with a kiss and then repeated on the other cheek. This is similar to the familiar men's greeting that we see some Europeans exchange with each other at times. As I observed and exchanged this greeting with Galib, I learned that you don't actually kiss each other's cheeks but contact cheek to cheek and pop your lips. This seemed to always start with the right cheek, and if you haven't seen each other in a while, then three or four times of cheek to cheek was the custom. So, every morning, as I greeted all the guys, I gave Galib his customary greeting in the workshop. Mohammad's guys got a kick out of me coming over to their shop in the morning, extending greetings to everyone, kissing Galib per Hilla custom, and prompting them to charge up and get to work. Everyone looked forward to the morning ritual. It was a great start of the day, and there were smiling faces everywhere. As time passed on, I was just as enthused about our morning greetings as they were.

I guess the word got out that I was a character and enthusiastic. And I was getting a little Arabic vocabulary built up and practicing with the guys during the workday. There began to be a lot of activity around the tool room and workshop throughout the day. More men would stop by to meet me and see how we were doing with the machinery rebuild. I was introduced to many friends of the guys. Galib and Mohammad helped with the English, and plenty of the guys were around to help with the Arabic, so much so that I soon had another Arabic word to add to my vocabulary. That word was "*caa-fee*," which means "enough." The guys taught me Arabic faster than my brain circuits could absorb. I settled in on a few key words and phrases because by then I was saturated. A small, pocket-sized, spiral-wound notepad was in my pocket at all times, and I began to take notes whenever possible. The guys would help me pronounce something, then point to my pants pocket for me to remove my little book and write it down.

Before only a few days had gone by, I knew the guys' names and abilities and even could give a few directions without Mohammad or Galib being right there. Malik would stop by often to check on us and help me along where he could. Mohammad had a counterpart named Omar who would work with us on certain equipment, and he had supervision of another entire crew. Omar was tall like Malik, was in his late thirties, and had a deep voice with English skills that might have exceeded Malik. He was a master at large, diesel engine rebuilding. Unfortunately, his skills came under scrutiny by Bruce on several occasions. Without having an in-depth assessment of Omar's skills, I went to bat for him and insisted on some trust be given to his crew. As it turned out, I believe that Omar was skeptical of us and rightly so. The assignment of a young, single American as the site leader, the promise of parts and tooling, and an ambitious schedule probably came across to him as an unworkable combination. Getting to know all of Omar's crew was difficult for me also because of the intermittent shoulder-to-shoulder work time I spent with them. Nevertheless, there were always smiles and waves as they would cross my path throughout the day.

One of the outstanding workers in the Omar crew was Tariq. He was an enthusiastic and reliable worker with a good grasp of English. Within the first day of meeting Tariq, I was told that he was one of the few that was granted a second wife by the local cleric. Tariq confirmed this to me and gave me a rough breakdown of the process of how this worked in his case. Tariq's first wife could not bear children. The local cleric noted this circumstance and eventually counseled Tariq to marry again. Since Shiites and Sunnis practice a form of arranged marriage, there are many candidates for the parents to recommend and Tariq to choose from. The first wife had to agree to this proposition. Typically, the first wife leaves her parents household to live with the husband and establish that household. As Tariq gained financial independence, he and his first wife established their own house. If the parents desire it, they can come and live with Tariq and abandon their household to one of Tariq's brothers. In Tariq's case, I believe they hadn't done this. Also, if I understood correctly, this is an option based on financial condition. The second wife usually stays with her parents and never leaves the household where she was raised to form a household with her husband. She raises the children with the help of her parents and any other of her siblings that are in that household still. There were other instances of polygamy that I learned about, and the basic structure seemed to be the same—usually a two-household arrangement with plenty of support from family members. From what I understand about Tariq's marriages, the second wife was in response to counsel from his local cleric. In another polygamous marriage I learned about, it was more of a personal choice of the husband and wife that was then approved by parents before being brought before the local religious authority for counsel.

If I understood correctly, the basic facts about Iraqi plural marriage are that they are lawful contracts, there is parental and religious involvement, it works as a plural household system, and it isn't widely practiced. One of the workers and I struggled through a conversation about this one day as he explained that in families or tribes that have a history of polygamy, it's likely that the practice continues today. There is extensive family involvement, but in Iraq, it is not like the arranged marriages as practiced in Pakistan, for instance. It also seems that the process can differ from one tribal region to another regarding clerical involvement versus tribal involvement. Working and talking with the mostly Shiite men, I got the perspective from that sector of Iraqi society. All I could find out about the Sunni side concerning this principle was that it is similar and conforms to Iraqi law and customs. Talking with some of our security men who had been in different regions of Iraq, they likened it to a tool to provide some harmony to the tribal societies for those who practiced it.

Because of Tariq's marital status, he earned the nickname "Two Wives" from me and the other Westerners. He would always greet me with a firm slap of the hand in the morning and was always anxious to pursue any work assignments given to him. In fact, Tariq's firm slap of the hand became more of a torture ritual between him and me every day. On certain occasions, I avoided him so I could recover from the previous day's hand slap. But all of us appreciated his reliability and admired his work ethic. Never would Tariq ever violate the sanctity of his marriages and discuss or even refer to any of the details of how he conducted himself in regard to physical intimacy with these two households. This was a welcome attribute I discovered that the Iraqi men shared and was a far cry from the cover-my-ears approach I needed with some of my Western colleagues.

Many of the other guys had their specific characteristic and a story. Chalupe was one of the taller men who was in his early fifties and was proud of his recent trip to Shiite holy sites in Iran. He would read some kind of prayer card or maybe a patriarchal blessing-type document bound into a booklet with pictures from his trip in early 2004. There was no shyness in him when he asked me to come sit down next to him in the workshop as he would flip through the pictures for me. This trip might have been significant to him because of the spiritual aspect of going to this Iranian Shiite holy site for the first time. He had fought in the Iran-Iraq war and spent time in Iran as a prisoner of war for several years. Having been able to go back to Iran to visit sacred shrines was a monumental occasion for him that he probably never expected would be possible. It seems that there is some form of reading done by a local religious authority near the shrine, and it is considered a blessing to be present. I tried to learn more specifics about the trip from him, but as usual, we fought through the language barrier for the details. Not understanding fully as usual, I stopped my full court press for information in order to be polite.

Chalupe was always a hard worker, thought things out before doing them, and looked out for me. He would come check on me every so often if I was looking at parts or was away from the machinery. He was always willing to seek me out and say, "Mark, *habibi, shlow-neck?*" which means "Mark, my friend, how are you?" He learned enough English for my sake to ask after my family and if I talked to them the night before. I would respond with "*Ze-en, shook-run,*" which means, "Fine, thank you," and try to ask about his family in return. As with all the guys, it's easy for me to envision Chalupe and myself sitting down and discussing the plan of salvation or just sharing stories about our children and engaging in small talk. Just as I would eventually discover with all the guys, there was a connection between us that I really couldn't explain.

Ahmed and Ayad were the two jokesters in the crew. Both spoke a limited amount of English. Ahmed was in his mid-twenties, and Ayad, mid-thirties. They both were married with small children at home. If anyone were going to convince me to hide a tool from someone or jokingly accuse someone of being Ali-Baba and taking my flashlight, these two guys were the conspirators. Ahmed was one of those types where his eyes would squint, and his entire facial features would be consumed in the process of smiling. He ended up being the guardian of our one precision measuring instrument that I had sent over from Kuwait. Since this precious, handheld, digital ruler known as a dial caliper was the only one available, Ahmed would keep it locked up in the workshop and retrieve it whenever necessary. Being the invaluable tool that it was, Ahmed took over the protection duties and carried them out flawlessly. After getting used to this arrangement, I would yell for Ahmed and he would hustle back to the workshop area to get the tool. It made it easy on me, and I didn't have to add another Arabic word to my easily forgotten vocabulary. The guys got a kick out of this experience as well. I would yell for Ahmed, then they would yell for Ahmed also to let him know that I needed the tool. Everyone would jump on the bandwagon, yelling above the background noise for Ahmed. As I would look around, there were smiles and snickers as Ahmed trotted off to fetch the tool. Upon the triumphant return with tool in hand, Ahmed would be in that full-facial smile as all his work buddies scolded him for taking so long. This scene repeated itself many times.

It was interesting to me to note that for Ahmed with responsibility came accountability. Ahmed freely took the responsibility as the dial indicator steward. Yet the others, including myself, held him accountable for the execution of those duties. We were depending on Ahmed to carry out that task so we could complete ours. When we agree or commit ourselves to perform a service or supply a product, others depend on us. In a gospel analogy, I couldn't help but think about church duties and duties within our own households. We depend on others to perform a task, but do we harshly hold them accountable? Maybe with some scrutiny and contempt? Or do we appreciate the effort and communicate gratitude and encouragement?

Ahmed's peers teased him a bit for being the tool-keeper, but we all came to depend and trust on him to carry out that duty.

In the overall view, I noticed that the guys appreciated Ahmed for this task and his willingness to perform without gripe or complaint. I could tell by their tone that they appreciated Ahmed and his contribution to the team. I never worried that this tool would get broken, lost, or stolen while he was the custodian. I've had this same type of tool come up missing so many times on other jobs I've done in the US and elsewhere. Alibaba doesn't reside only in Iraq. Ahmed showed an admirable display of responsibility for such a basic task. The simple things many of us could learn from such a serving spirit like Ahmed.

Ayad, the other jokester, was known for his abundant talking. Although I didn't know what he was saying, he always seemed to have a point to make and liked to get in the last word. He also had an amazing story. He had spent two years in prison for bad-mouthing Saddam. Apparently, there were specialists in each area of the country to monitor public opposition to the regime. Ayad spoke poorly of Saddam in public one day and word got back to the official channels. He was sentenced to ten years in prison but only served two. He proudly displayed his "political prisoner" ID card to me several times. The card was in Arabic but had "political prisoner" in English in black letters at the top. It may have been from Amnesty International or some other recognized organization, but I couldn't tell.

After being imprisoned for two years, I would have expected Ayad to still be a little embittered. Actually, it was just the opposite. He was released just before the March 2003 invasion and his outlook on life was quite positive, as was his work ethic and his ability to interact with his co-workers. There was no mention of the torture or any type of mental abuse that he had been subjected to, just the loss of two years of his life. Sometimes I think these men put the pain out of their minds somehow and just focused on the future and their current blessings . I marvel at the upbeat personality Ayad has, considering all he had been through.

The rest of the guys were just as pleasant to be around. Adnan was in his early thirties, knew very little English, and was always anxious to learn. Jwad was the computer geek and liked to sneak over to our office trailer to check out my laptop. Ayad and Jwad managed to get me to do a computer search for a famous portrait of Imam Ali in a digital format and print out a copy for them. It wasn't a great copy, but they were satisfied regardless. I saved the digital file and made some personal plans for this picture for the future. Jwad showed off his computer talent to me when he presented me with a copy of a fancy collage of pictures from our project on a computer program. He had gotten copies on diskette of some digital pictures some of the security men were taking and composed a slide show out of them. When he brought the copy over for me on CD, I didn't know what to expect. It was in an older file format but was still quite impressive. It was well done with graphics and music and lasted for over thirty minutes. Since Jwad was one of the younger men in the crew, it made sense that he was computer literate. He had taught himself recently, since computers were out of financial bounds for most of the men and difficult to obtain in the local markets.

Maithaim was another of the young guys that worked hard and talked fast. Sometimes he would stutter getting the words out because he was so anxious to contribute. There was another Mohammad in the crew. He was on the labor side with the rest of the guys. Since there were two Mohammads I would be dealing with, I named the two guys Mohammad One and Mohammad Two. Whenever I would need one or the other, I would just say "Mohammad One?" or "Mohammad Two?" and hold up one or two fingers. Mohammad Two was in his mid-to-late thirties, had small children at home, and spoke some English. He had a cautious type of approach to things and was careful using tools and equipment. I learned that he had been working there for over sixteen years and still couldn't afford to buy his own house. The guys told me that under Saddam the average pay for the working-class Iraqi was an equivalent of about three US dollars a month. Today, they were getting more like two US dollars an hour.

There were two men named Satar, so they also got nick-named "Satar One" and "Satar Two." Both were in their early thirties with small children at home. Satar One had a fair English vocabulary and was another thinker-worker as most of the guys were. I was impressed with how they were all contin-ually thinking of better and safer ways to perform a task, not just doing as directed. Satar Two was a little more on the quiet side. He had only a few English words in his vocabulary and was kind of shy. Several times in the beginning he would opt out of any pictures I would take. Eventually, I learned that he was one of those pessimistic-type personalities. As time went by, he softened up and even smiled and posed as I was snapping the rest of the gang throughout the workday.

Weesam was the final character in our tightly bonded crew. Because of Weesam, I learned the Arabic word for happy which is "sa'eed." Another one of the younger guys, Weesam always had a smile on his face. He was married, and his wife had a baby boy while we were there. Just as the other guys would tease Ahmed for being the tool guardian, Ayad for talking too much, and Matthaim for stuttering, Weesam was poked at because he was always happy. A few days after the birth of his son, Weesam was gone from work for the day. When I inquired about it, the guys explained that the baby was getting circumcised. I'd never thought about Islamic teachings in regard to circumcision. Apparently, it's done in the home with a religious authority and a medial practitioner present. It is a family event with close friends invited by the household. The procedure is performed in a ceremonial manner after which there is a celebration with food and socializing. I never found out if there was any timing factor such as with the Jewish custom of the eighth day. But I did learn that the Koran does not specifically command the practice; rather, it is a custom from the Prophet Muhammad and Imam Ali.

There were many others that would stop by the worksite throughout the day, offer a greeting, and be on their way. Some were indirectly involved in the project and liked to see what we were doing. All in all, there were about eighteen men whose names I eventually learned and remembered, and another six or eight that I saw daily and acknowledged with a wave or a handshake. To help you picture the gregarious nature of these men, imagine this: Every morning before work the entire staff met together and personally greeted one another. Handshakes, kisses, and pats on the back were everywhere. Before lunch they all came together, spread their mats on the floor, and took turns saying their prayers. They socialized a bit during the prayer time. I found out that it was not rude to talk and continue business with bystanders while others were in the midst of their prayer cycle. However, I made it a practice to step away if I was in the area to be reverent. After completing prayers, they rolled out the eating mat and put out their home-cooked best to share lunch. No one ate individual meals; instead, they put it all out on the rug for all to partake. Everything was then picked up, cleaned, and stowed away in a communal fashion. Every workday was like a ward activity. All the elements were there: greetings, socialization, prayers, food and sharing of food, team clean up, and conclusion. I enjoyed their company and would eventually accept their lunch offers many times. Despite the language difficulty, we communicated tolerably well and shared small talk, laughs, and cultural exchange throughout the entire workday. The noon meal would be the forum where we would learn the most details about each other.

But most of my experience and discussion was with the men and not many women. There were many women working at the plant, and one young woman engineer was assigned to our electrical activities. She and I would make eye contact and say "Hello" in English whenever she was in the area. No handshakes or touching is the custom. Without knowing this,

I still always kept a gentlemanly distance. Once again, I was abiding by a culture principle out of gospel standards and common sense. Basically, the guys didn't initiate much talk about the women. I would refer to their wives getting mad at them for smoking too much or that their wife might pound them for ruining nice work clothes. They all accepted the humorous references and agreed that there was a tight line to walk within their households. But otherwise, they didn't get into details about their wives, their sisters, or female work associates to any great extent. Instead, they prized their children, especially their boys, and talked about them. When they found out that my firstborn was a boy, they quickly remembered his name, and from then on, it was a daily occurrence for them to ask me "How is David?" even before they asked about my wife and the rest of the family. They knew I would talk on the phone in the evening to the family back home every other day or so. They quickly remembered all my children's names and would ask me about them daily. But I think there is a stereotype here. The impression I got was that this reluctance to discuss details about wives and other women did not seem to be a superiority issue or a form of male chauvinism. It seemed more of a reverence to women by keeping them out of male conversation. Perhaps similar to our somewhat mute acknowledgement of a Heavenly Mother. Disgrace and disparagement are avoided by keeping the maternal side of our Heavenly Parents removed from the conversation.

In just a little over a week I had gotten to know the plant workers and their management, and we were educating each other on cultural issues at a phenomenal pace. I continued to wave and shake lots of hands in the morning. As I attended the morning greeting festivities, I noticed an additional gesture offered by my Iraqi friends. After a handshake and shoulder bump, the guys would step back and put their right hand over their heart and slightly bow their head. Even the men that would walk by the office trailer in the morning would do this after I offered a quick wave and a smile as a greeting. I asked about the meaning of this gesture. The interpretation was not a surprise. Just as the gesture demonstrates, it means "from the heart" or "with great respect." It wasn't just for me that they would offer this utmost form of greeting. Sure, I tried to act proper, friendly, and helpful. But it was really the overall scheme that earned us this high form of appreciation for our presence there. To the Iraqis, it was an honor to have men from nations of freedom and liberty come to their aid. We brought with us tools, skills, knowledge, and techniques they were deprived of for decades. We also brought guards, guns, and armored vehicles. But it wasn't to force them to comply or terrorize them into submission. It was to protect us from deadly opposition and assure them that we could continue our task to increase power production for their benefit.

How did I know these people really appreciated our help and our presence there? Along with the heartfelt greetings and warm smiles of acceptance, there were several other experiences that indicated gratitude. One incident occurred during the first few days onsite. A local delivery vehicle pulled over near our office. They needed to verify directions with some of our workers nearby. As I walked up with my security guard to see if the package was for our job, the driver anxiously engaged me with some broken English. He asked if I was American or British. When I told him American, he grabbed my hand and said, "Thank you for Mr. Bush, thank you." He then labored through the communication to ensure that I was going to vote for Mr. Bush in November, and he offered an analogy of the candidates. For Mr. Bush, he said, "He looks straight ahead," for Mr. Kerry, "He looks down at his feet." To me, this was simple to interpret. President Bush had a forward-looking vision and Senator Kerry looked at the present. I gladly assured him we were there to help and would not leave. He thanked me profusely and left.

I had been working with the guys for about two weeks now and had been through a whirlwind of cultural and social exposure. The threat of incoming mortar rounds had already been served one evening in camp, so I got practiced in the art of scrambling to the nearby cement bunker without delay. Overall, the "jittery factor" was still high for me. There was another project similar to ours near the Coalition base. We shared the camp, the security team, and the contract. Since the machinery was similar, we would borrow components as needed until replacements would arrive.

One day, we needed to deliver a component to the other site before heading to our facility. Having never been to the other project, I was anxious to see the plant, the people, and the work environment. The other site was a quick trip within easy reach of the base. The visit was short and to the point. I dropped off the parts, took a quick look around, said some hellos, and headed out the front gate. We were in our usual four-vehicle convoy this morning, and I was in the second vehicle. On a typical trip, the distance between each vehicle could vary from bumper to bumper to as much as 100 yards. There was about forty yards between each of us as we slowed down to negotiate some rough roads. We were less than a quarter mile from the plant gate. Right at the point of slowest travel, a roadside bomb was detonated almost exactly between the first vehicle and ours. The concussion instantaneously rocked our vehicle, and an immediate cloud of dust turned day into night. Our driver and front seat lookout acted promptly and shouted into his radio for all vehicles to "GO! GO! GO!" We raced through the blinding dust as fast as possible. Ikram and I were the only passengers in the rear seat of our vehicle. We both clasped our hands together tightly, held our breath, bowed our heads, and closed our eyes briefly as in a prayer. Our security team rushed the vehicle convoy out of the area. We drove on the brink of control in a roundabout fashion back to the safety of the Coalition base. Radio traffic went wild. We had just survived a "contact" event. Fortunately, it was a miss.

CHAPTER 7

The experience of a roadside bomb is impossible to put into words. My ears were ringing for hours. We were fortunate to have had some distance between us and the bomb and the ability to drive away. Timing is key to the success or failure of the device.

Later, some of our security contractors told us to look for perpetrators in parked cars and watch the children in the future. We were used to the children running up to the road and giving the thumbs-up as we drove by on a daily basis. Our security men explained to us that it's possible for local children to sometimes give a thumbs-down signal as a warning that suspicious activity has taken place. This was just one of several remarkable pieces of information our security contractors would relay to us. One specific account was that of a private security team operating north of Baghdad in unfamiliar territory. The kids were running up and giving the thumbs-down to them. The team just thought these kids were rude. They continued to drive and were narrowly missed by a road bomb a short distance away. After consulting with counterpart security teams familiar to that area, they discovered the children were giving them the warning sign. It was a common communication tool used between the locals, the Coalition forces, and the contractors in that area. In other areas of the country, Coalition forces and private security teams would notice the adults avoiding eye contact if insurgents were around. When the coast was clear, it was back to friendly eye contact and smiling as teams would drive by.

Fortunately for us, this device missed the target—which was probably any Coalition forces or Western vehicles. But the demoralizing effect was substantial. We were in a lockdown status on the Coalition base for four days. Visualize four days of scared men continually talking, speculating, and theorizing about the event. Sort of like the game where you pass the story around and then compare the final version to the original. The perception was getting skewed, and an unfounded mistrust of our private security contractor began to develop. Regardless of the reason, a bomb went off that could have killed or maimed any of us. It was a lesson in reality that all of Iraq is dangerous and security measures should not be allowed to get complacent. One engineer from each project quit and went home. We were all free to leave at any time, and discussion was rampant throughout our team about doing so. The final consensus was that this was a random act, the armored vehicles do provide safety, and we should be able to continue the work without further danger. Since our site was in a different direction from the base, it was easier to rationalize our safety and continue the work. So, the plan was set, and after being away for four days, we returned to work, minus the one electrical engineer from our project. There was some communication between Malik and Brent during our absence, but I wasn't privy to any details. I wasn't sure all the plant workers knew the reason we weren't there.

Loading up and driving out that next morning was as reverent as a funeral. Usually there's some chatter while we get going and drive out to the site. That morning there was some breath holding going on instead. When we arrived through the plant gates and at our work trailer, we eased up a bit and started to talk. It was different with one of us gone now, and it was a constant reminder of the reality of the event. Sometimes our minds tend to take traumatic events and displace them so as not to impair our ability to function. I can honestly say that I had a difficult time focusing on the work for several days. Before, there was a comfort level that all of us achieved that allowed us to focus in on our tasks and solve problems. With the reminder of the fragile nature of mortality still fresh, each of us started off at a toned-down pace with a cautious attitude.

I wasn't even thinking about the guys as I walked up to the workshop to see what was going on. The "Salaam Alikum" ritual was out of my mind, and I was trying to sort out feelings about work, life, and gospel principles. It became real to me that many of our young soldiers had been killed in this country, and I dwelled on how their families must grieve for their loss. My mind raced with thoughts about how to avoid any indication of danger when talking to my wife back home. Walking into the workshop, I surprised the guys as they were talking in a serious manner. There was a flurry of activity as everyone surrounded me, and we started to struggle through the communications. We didn't go through our normal greetings. Instead, there was just an onrush of men that became larger as the workshop filled with others from outside that I didn't even know. Someone went and got Malik, and he walked in and took over the conversation. It all got quiet. They had a solemn concern about us, and they wanted to make sure that we were okay. I explained that one of our team opted to return home and that the rest of us wanted to finish the project as best we could. They were worried about any of us getting hurt or killed. At this point, Malik put his hand on my shoulder and said that Allah had protected our team of contractors, and they were all praying for each of us every day since they heard the news. The plant workers were glad to hear that we were okay and that we had chosen to stay and help.

It was so humbling to have these men of another faith and culture express sincere concern and tell me they were praying for us to their God. I could tell this wasn't a shallow emotion for them. This was genuine. One by one, the men took my hand in a handshake gesture and pulled me in for a quick bear-hug-type grasp. Galib kissed each of my cheeks twice at least and walked away with his eyes welled up in tears. As the crowd started to disperse, most of the men drifted back into serious debate among themselves. Without knowing what they were saying, I could tell one thing from their tone: they were sick of the attacks. As the days went on, Malik, Galib, and Mohammad were sure to let me know that these insurgent attacks were not local men from nearby towns or anywhere close. Greeting everyone in the mornings was something that only I did with the work crew, so I believe I was the only one of us to experience this circle of concern that first morning back at the plant. But the trepidation from Malik and the plant staff was for all of us. They were sad to hear one of us had left, but they were grateful that everyone was safe.

Fear subsided, and things settled after a few days. We got back into a routine. I started back into the business of working with the guys and getting their machinery put back together. Work progress had tapered off due to a lack of specific tools, so I was trying to get the preparatory work done to fill in. The outside temperature had hovered in the 120°F range for several days in a row. It was hard to motivate the workers and myself after their prayers and lunch hour. One of the critical tasks was drilling many holes into a hardened steel component. Because of the critical nature and the lack of spare parts, I couldn't afford a mistake, so I got right in there with them. Most of the other guys were doing parts cleaning tasks, so I was only with a few of the men while we drilled these holes. As I worked more closely with these few men, I saw that they had been deprived of some basic skillsets that a mechanical technician should have. But it was more an issue of tooling and practices. They just didn't have the exposure to functional equipment that we in the Westernized world were accustomed to in the industry. At one point, we were seizing our precious lone drill bit during use and threatening to damage it. Since high-grade drill bits were not available locally, ruining the bit was not an option. A simple method of careful drilling calls for using a slower drill speed with lubrication such as WD-40. As I worked through the motions and did some basic demonstrations, I realized that the guys probably hadn't used a variable-speed, electric hand drill before. As we progressed more into this task, I showed them that the drill had a reverse direction if needed, and this feature could be used for removing a seized drill bit. They didn't realize the full features of the tool, but the guys caught on quickly.

During our evening walk on the base, it tired me to listen to some of the other contractors criticize these people for not having standard skills that we were accustomed to in the US and other advanced countries. The implication was that our workers were stupid. My assertion was that they are ignorant. I tried to explain that there is a difference between ignorance and stupidity. Being ignorant is not a bad thing and can be out of one's control. Part of our directives from the US government representative was to teach and train the labor force as we assembled the machinery. How was this forgotten? The plant guys were diligent but uninformed. I'm not sure how far I got with the defense. I really did start feeling sorry for those that held corporate leadership responsibility. Iraq was such a harsh working environment and so disconnected from the modern world. Yet pressure from corporate people in faraway, air-conditioned offices was increasing. There should have been more restraint and understanding of the roadblocks to progress, especially in Iraq or other areas with extraordinary logistical and humanitarian conditions. Younger professionals tend to respond more dramatically to corporate pressure, so I had sympathy for Brent and the other leaders having to justify and explain every delay or obstacle. So now both groups were getting pressured— the plant guys for work practices and corporate leadership for work progress.

By now I was a getting a little disturbed at Brent and his corporate captains applying the pressure. When the director general of the entire facility visited our office trailer one afternoon, it seemed that good etiquette was thrown out the window. Everything got quiet when Malik brought this distinguished Iraqi man into the office trailer, and Brent would not break the ice with any small talk or gracious offerings. There were a couple security guards, along with Brent and me, in the trailer at the time. The director general spoke excellent English and offered all of us firm handshakes and greetings of "Hello, how are you?" before we offered him a seat. Malik tried to keep conversation going, but it was somewhat one-sided. When the director general realized he was going to get only minimal information from us, he then excused himself in a most professional manner, saying, "I see all is going well over here, so then I will leave you to your work." I probably didn't chime in as much as I could have, but I chose to defer that function to Brent as the appointed leader. Later, I softly chastised Brent for not rolling out the red carpet and for waiting to answer questions instead of initiating conversation with our important guest. I tried to explain how important it was to offer guests a soda, ask how their family is doing, offer to take them out to see the work progress, and make small talk. These are common courtesies and help breach the culture gap. It was an embarrassing episode, and I don't think Brent even understood what I was telling him.

But the matter of the tooling still bothered me. Perhaps these tools have been available in Iraq for the last several years and possibly cost and budget allocations of these struggling facilities did not allow the proper tooling to get into the proper hands. The lack of a drill bit, cutting tool, or bolt-threading tool could stop progress altogether. Local market purchases required cash transactions, and there was not any proper planning for this procedure at the time. For an industrialized country, there was an extreme lack of quality tooling and supplies that could be sourced. Several times we would see items missing from the equipment. When we asked Malik why they didn't replace this tool or why they didn't replace that item, he explained that the restrictions of the UN sanctions prohibited many items from being available. So, the plant was left to the ingenuity of their staff and the availability of the meager onsite spares to keep the equipment running. It was actually a testament to their resourcefulness. Being deprived so long of proper spares and tooling, these people kept things working to the best of their capability under incredibly difficult circumstances.

Malik took me into the warehouse and machine shop for the first time to look at their supplies. Walking through the machine shop portion was a return to a junkyard-type atmosphere again. Broken parts and rusted hulls of large, fabricated-steel vessels lay strewn about randomly. As we continued to the warehouse, the contrast between it and the machine shop was eye-opening. Here, the supplies were orderly, relatively clean, and structured in an efficient manner. There were several women working in the administration functions. Since women tend to be inherently better organized than men, this is always a plus and shows shrewd managerial planning and secular tolerance. It also showed me the independent nature of

Iraqi society. These are traits common to a capitalistic market economy.

Days were clicking by, and progress was slowed by heat and tooling needs. Our team had become a common fixture by now. Our private security men would converse, joke, and laugh with the plant workers and others that would come up to see how we were doing. One of our UK security men brought me a note from one of the plant workers he had been talking with. The man's name was Ali, and he was asking our guys to help him contact some long-lost friends in America. Since I was American, this got passed on to me. There was a certain level of excitement about the task, and I soon found out why. In the late sixties and early seventies, Ali's father had worked for some Jewish business owners in the region. With the toppling of power into the hands of Saddam, this entire Jewish family fled to America, somewhere in California. I was excited myself to meet Ali to discuss what I could do. Ali had good English skills and was grateful beyond measure that I would try to help make a connection. We went up into my office space in the trailer, and both sat down. Ali grabbed my hand and held it tightly as he thanked me over and over and talked excitedly about finding these great family friends. I felt a little weird at first about the hand holding, even though I realized that men holding hands is a cultural custom in the Middle East. Even President Bush took his media hits doing this with the Saudi prince in late April 2005 while strolling through the White House grounds.

Originally, I thought this would be an easy task: use the internet and do a search. But name changes, spelling deviations, and the amount of time since that family fled Iraq ended up complicating the search. I committed to Ali to find some kind of information for him. Although I had nothing to report to him right away, he would stop by my office space at least once a week, sit down, grab my hand, and discuss the optimistic future of Iraq now that Saddam's regime was gone. Many times, he repeated that now the people of his country needed to fix their internal conflicts. But he explained that he meant conflicts within the inside of each person. He meant their attitude and emotions. They needed to take pride and responsibility in their work, shun corrupt behavior, and distance themselves from the past. He knew they needed to clean up their landscape of the trash and debris left over from the oppressive years and start over. His simple explanation to me was they needed to heal from the wounds of tyranny. It was always a welcome visit when Ali would stop by every week or so. He was always excited and optimistic. I managed to turn Ali's request over to a more experienced public figure eventually, and I believe that there has been some recent progress made.

There always seemed to be someone with English skills stopping by and wanting to engage in talk. Our liaison with the US government entity was also named Ali. He was a young engineer in his mid-thirties and a local who spoke excellent English. We called him Al, and he'd stop by at least once a week to look around and check on the progress. Many times, he'd catch us in the trailer on break or checking email, sit down, and initiate conversation. He would ask technical questions, talk politics, share stories of the brutality of Saddam, discuss the potential of his country, explain cultural differences, and discuss world events. I always obliged him and enjoyed the education.

By this time, everyone had heard of some of the brutal exploits Saddam's sons were alleged to have committed, but Al elaborated. Without going into any graphic detail, Al explained that every Thursday you could not find a single woman on the streets of Baghdad because of these men. Saddam's sons would direct their personal guards to find a woman from off the street and bring her to an unknown location for personal pleasure. If the women were killed or not was never known. But Al told us this particular story because he said it demonstrated the insidious character of his nation's past leadership. He pleaded with us to know that the average Iraqi is a good person and was embarrassed by this behavior. Most Iraqis were thoroughly disgusted with the continued tolerance the world had of Saddam during those years. Al also had the vision of a new Iraq similar to Ali, recognizing that there needs to be a human healing period to adjust. In the weeks to come, Al would be the one to offer one of the most profound observations about our particular work and conduct there at that project.

I was starting to get a better picture of what some of these people had been through over the years. Back at camp in the evenings, I'd anxiously watch for any of the mainstream media reports coming from US or British sources on my room TV. In fact, most of us would turn our room TVs onto BBC or CNN International and leave them there for the entire evening. I gobbled up any news reports about Iraq because of the security concerns in our locations and the fascinating aspects of public opinion that had developed. It was interesting to see the negative news dominate. But to be fair, we didn't want anyone to broadcast the fact that we were in a rebuilding project getting electrical facilities back in operation. The contractors preferred the stealth approach to our project visibility because it kept us safer. I pondered on this for a couple of days and had come to a personal conclusion of how we should handle any press should they show up. We could just tell them that there was no bad news here and then they wouldn't be interested. That line of thinking predominated among most of us.

On September 23, we were treated to a live newscast of Interim Prime Minister Allawi giving an address to the US Congress at 12 p.m. Eastern Standard Time. It was around 8 p.m. local time for us, and our satellite TV network picked it up on the BBC. I watched intently in the privacy of my room and began to listen carefully to the content of the prime minister's address. As I choked back emotions from the thundering applause Congress gave at his appearance, I had a difficult time focusing on the latter part of his speech due to his opening. It was the beginning that stuck with me. He basically said thank you to the American people and the American government. He thanked us for our sacrifice and the sacrifice of lives on their behalf. To me, there was a humble tone in his voice. Being present on Iraqi soil as this historic speech took place gave me great satisfaction in our cause and made me feel proud to be an American. It was an honor to assist those who had lived under such tyranny and an honor to begin such great friendships with these Iraqi men I was working side by side with at this very moment.

Within a day or so of the Allawi speech, I saw a BBC news headline marquee blurb go by on a camp TV in the evening. It briefly said more mass graves found in Hilla, south of Baghdad. It caught my attention since I knew Galib was from there. The next day I gave my best attempt to solemnly inform Galib of the headline. He said he heard the news, but he wasn't up to talking about it. Already aware of Galib's soft heart, I wasn't surprised at his reaction to my inquiry. He walked away from me but stopped in his tracks after a foot. He turned and raised his right hand to his face, pointed to his eyes, and said, "With these eyes I have seen this before. I am sorry I cannot talk about this with you, Mark." He turned and walked away with his head lowered to the ground. I saw him wipe away tears a distance away before I turned and departed from the encounter. These headline news items weren't removed incidents, far from our lives and the rather surreal society that we know as Iraq; these were real people living with the consequences that brutal tyranny brought. My heart was so heavy for him that the entire episode numbed me for the rest of the day and into a restless sleep that evening.

There always seemed to be a balance to the interactions I experienced. Nobody sought us out just to detail how difficult their life had been. Malik was another one to come into the office trailer, sit down, and discuss and share cultural and religious values when the time allowed. His wife came in one day to meet us and even brought the younger of their two children with her. She was quite fair in appearance with not as dark a complexion as Malik. She wore some simple jewelry around her neck, no earrings, no perfume, and just some basic eye make-up, all of which gave me the impression that mother was her primary role. It was hard to tell with all the loose, robe-like clothing she wore, but she might have been a slight bit overweight. Along with the somewhat fancy head scarf, she wore a long, dark dress and a loose, wrist-length blouse that almost gave the appearance of a shawl. As she first ventured into our office space, she commented that this must be Mark and that must be Brent over there, speaking very clear English for all of us to hear. It was apparent that Malik had done plenty of talking about us at home, and his wife basically knew us sight unseen. Malik introduced her and their young toddler daughter to us, and we nodded our heads and said hello. In deference to local custom, we offered no handshakes.

She asked us about our families, where we were from, how many children we had, and so on. As I showed her some digital pictures of my wife and children on my laptop, she was particularly complementary of what a cute family I had and even joked that my house must be busy with four children. They were the typical questions and comments a married woman with children would have asked. Her conduct and character conveyed her status as a distinguished, middle-aged woman and a person that others in their society respect and graciously accept her counsel as wisdom. At no time did Malik do the talking for her or take control of the conversation. Actually, Malik and I had many conversations concerning our personal, spouse-influenced conduct while at home. And I had the same verbal exchanges with Mohammad, Galib, and all the guys. We would joke together often about treading on eggshells with our wives when at home and how difficult it was to get our spouses off the phone when they were engaged in conversations with other women. And, of course, the universal man-complaint of too much time spent in the market just browsing or overspending. It was another one of those many cultural intersections that we shared. Departure time came quickly, and she left some home-cooked goodies for us. She was employed elsewhere in the plant and had to return the little girl back to the organized daycare facility located somewhere nearby. We made sure to stuff the little girl's pockets with candies, so everybody left with a smile.

A few days later, Malik brought in a photo album to show us some pictures of him and friends during their college years, visiting with each other in Baghdad. Most of the pictures were old and graying and showed their 1970s vintage. Many photos had them in groups of people with a mix of guys and girls. These were his courtship days, and there appeared to be many ladies available. Many of the photos were taken at some kind of theme park with Ferris wheels and a petting zoo. Malik explained to me the principles of courtship and arranged marriage as they practice it. I wasn't too surprised to learn that their society separates the girls from the boys all the way through the high school age years, then co-ed was allowed in college. From the school children we would drive by when traveling from the camp to the plant, I always noticed they were either all boys or all girls. I couldn't recall any mixed group.

The arranged marriage principle intrigued me. As he explained more, I realized it wasn't a truly arranged situation where partners were matched up solely on parental decree.

Parents would often arrange blind dates for their offspring with other parents they knew through social networks. I actually thought it was a great plan. If my kids would only date other kids their mother and I selected, the stresses of parenting could be tapered down a bit. But the Iraqi system gets even better. If young adults meet others outside of that parental boundary, a simple social meeting of the parents is held, and each set of parents must approve of the potential in-laws before any discussion of marriage continues. Of course, there are cases where this is violated. Malik and I mused at how love can frequently be the confounder of order. But the whole principle was based on the respect of parental approval. Honor thy Father and Mother that thy days may be long on the Earth. It was one of many great cultural exchanges that took place, and I would grow to respect their society even more through the process of understanding.

The next few days got exciting as hostilities began between the Muqtada Al-Sadr militia and British troops in Basra. The topic of the militias dominated our conversations for the next couple days. All the guys would firmly tell me "Al-Sadr moo-rah-ha," meaning "Al-Sadr no good." As for how the plant workers felt about militias, it was clear. The men told me that the Al-Sadr militia was not welcome in any of the region by the locals, and the plant workers communicated to me that they were hoping for a defeat this time. Mohammad and Galib told me that about thirty-five plant employees were discovered to be in the Al-Sadr militia, and they were immediately fired.

There were plenty of military jets ripping through the skies for a few days. Malik told us his two young girls were scared and slept tightly with Mommy and Daddy for the few nights while jet noise roared off and on. Malik's biggest concern was how to know when it was completely over. But what he said next caught my attention. What he was looking for was the communication similar to that during the initial invasion in 2003. I queried him a little further and got some details. When President Bush declared from the USS *Lincoln* on May 3 that "major combat operations in Iraq have ended," the Iraqi people received the statement as a clearance call. With that declaration, they knew that deadly bombs and armaments would no longer be used. That was their indication that it was now safe to come out of their homes and hiding places. And they did. Malik told me after that message was given people knew it was safe and ventured out. I never did find out how they got that message. Were there Iraqi radio stations working? Was it blared over loudspeakers from a mosque? But the concept of a clearance signal for citizens never even occurred to me.

My recall of that event was how the US media played that one out as a miscalculation of the US president and our military leaders. I recalled how day after day, our national media announced yet another American military death in Iraq, then inserted a count of how many days had passed since the president announced major hostilities had ended in Iraq. What an amazing revelation to know the locals believed and trusted the American president. As I went through that entire scenario from Malik's viewpoint, it just made sense. The Basra hostilities eventually ceased, and we never heard much more about the Al-Sadr militia after those September hostilities.

As with most of the men, Malik had a spiritual side he was not timid to share. He would come into the office in the middle of crude jokes or discussion by the security guys and others and would politely hold his dignity and conduct his business. I caught him in a deep spiritual discussion with Brent one afternoon. As I listened in, I realized that Malik wasn't trying to convert him; instead, he was explaining principles of repentance. He was trying to explain mortal expectations from God and "save" our wayward young site leader from his sins of excess.

Sometimes Malik would gravitate over toward me or Ikram, our Pakistani engineer, to engage in small talk or ask questions. I continually reminded myself of the sensitive nature of our work in Iraq but always felt good about sharing cultural values. These became great opportunities to discuss some basic gospel principles with Malik because he was curious. Why was I different? Malik knew I didn't drink and smoke, and I didn't engage in sexual talk like most of the others. I was checking email on my laptop while the guys were on one of their breaks. Malik was in the office and came over to my desk and sat down. I went over to the LDS.org website and showed him pictures of temples from all over the world. My intent was to show him the worldwide nature of the Church and use the temples to demonstrate the expanse of our religion. I briefly explained the First Vision, the importance of the Book of Mormon to us and the world, and why it was significant to me along with the joy and blessings living the commandments had given me and my family.

I had two Arabic copies of the Book of Mormon with me. They were on top of a small file cabinet in a corner of my work area. When I showed him the cover, he picked it up and flipped through it some while we talked. He asked questions regarding the hierarchy and structure within the Church, and he also seemed to be trying to clarify and relate the structure of the Catholic Church to our own. There is a Catholic population in the region, and Malik must have had some exposure to Christianity through them. He put the Arabic Book of Mormon back on my file cabinet after glancing through it. I was dying for him to ask if he could have it or borrow it for more study.

But we got into a deeper discussion I didn't expect with some surprising Islamic doctrine I was not aware of. We talked about the relationship of Abraham to Islam, Judaism, and Christianity and that all three have roots back to Abraham. For Malik, this in effect says we worship the same God. Malik then explained to me that it was Abraham who said that all who worshipped his (Abraham's) god were considered Muslims. Malik shared that he was a Sunni Muslim, and there are some differing beliefs between them and the Shiite Muslims. One difference he offered to share with me at that point was the fact that Sunni Muslims do not try to portray the Prophet Muhammad or any other historical religious figure in paintings or portraits. He shared other small details that I forgot soon after because the Abraham-Muslim thing was reeling back and forth in my mind this whole time. I wondered how he came up with that idea? Where in his scripture was that located? Did they have other writings they believed were from Abraham, or was everything passed down through the Prophet Muhammad? But Malik could have been off track on the Abraham-Muslim issue. Just as differing Christian congregations have different beliefs, Malik's religious training might have a doctrinal belief that wasn't in the mainstream or he had a misconception. Regardless, it would be interesting to pursue at a different level and discover the root of this belief.

After my religious discussion with Malik that day, my intention with the guys was to try to educate them a little more about the differing Christian faiths and why my life was different because of my Church membership. A close ward member and I were in email discussions of how I would approach the Book of Mormon distribution issue. I had come in possession of these two hardbound Arabic editions years ago and had packed them in with my gear with the hope that I would be able to give them out eventually in Iraq. Not knowing any specific rules or guidelines for conduct regarding proselytizing after arriving in Iraq, I became a little more cautious. After some emails back and forth to my ward friend, I had a somewhat better guideline. And it made sense. Apparently, there had been several inquiries to Church leadership about this eventuality from military members. The counsel my friend shared with me was to give out copies of the Book of Mormon if local nationals asked. In other words, I shouldn't just hand them out but wait until I was asked. I had done the proper thing with Malik when I refrained from offering it to him.

So, I took a different approach for the future. I brought out both Arabic copies and left them in the open where I worked throughout the day researching and labeling parts for the plant. The guys would always come around to see how I was doing with the parts research, then come over to visit during their break period if I wasn't with them on the machinery. Actually, I think the parts area became a mini social center, and the guys would come over during their break period to visit often. My sister had sent me a beginner's Arabic-to-English phrasebook for reference that had become a big hit and was always getting passed around by the guys. So, I left everything out in the open.

Galib was the first one to take notice and asked what Arabic book I had. I told him this was my holy book, and I was using it to compare the Arabic writing to the Arabic-English phrasebook. He looked through it and read the title page and introduction. What happened next floored me! He said something like, "That's what happened to those people." He'd caught my attention, and I engaged in conversation. Though I was trying to be casual about this experience, I was really chomping at the bit for feedback.

Galib had read about the Jaredites in the introduction. He couldn't pronounce Palestine, so we went round and round trying to figure out what he meant. Then, he told me this group was taken away captive by "Korash" and into Palestine near the time of the confusion of the tongues at Babylon. I pressed him on the pronunciation of "Korash" a few times but tried not to be rude. What was so profound to me was not that the history he knew was different than the account recorded in Ether, it was the fact that his history acknowledged that a group of people were displaced from Babylon in that time period. Since Galib spent time as a tour guide in Babylon, I thought his recollection of the history could be valid. But he could be wrong, his memory fading as the years went by or from a bad piece of initial historical information to begin with. Regardless, the encounter of the subject brought goose bumps to my spine. That evening I frantically looked for any mention of "Korash" in the scriptures. I found a mention of Korash in the Pearl of Great Price in Facsimile 2, but no details. These are investigations the late Dr. Hugh Nibley would have been capable of dealing with.

The end result of our conversation was that Galib took the book and ended up reading the entire book of Ether (or most of it). He never asked any more questions but commented that it was very good. The bulk of the other guys came over during that occasion and got into the discussion. Since I had the second Arabic Book of Mormon sitting there, I offered it out to read, and it was passed around and discussed. At one point more than half the work crew crowded into my parts inventory area and engaged in a heated discussion over my holy book. They passed it from one to another and debated loudly. The saddest part of this whole episode was that I didn't know what they were saying. Were they pleased? Were they offended? The claim of another "*Nebi*" (Arabic for "prophet") outside of Muhammad was supposed to be offensive to them. Were they going to ask their local cleric about this? Was the local cleric going to come find me and confront me? I started to get a little paranoid. There was a small commotion going on because of me. Things died down after that incident, but Chalupe ended up coming over several times in the next day or so to read from my holy book for a few minutes at a time during his breaks. After he had his fill, he handed it back to me and said "Mark, this holy book is very good." Wow, I absolutely didn't know what these guys thought about all this. I just left the books sitting in their original spot. I actually felt some relief when the whole episode appeared over. I just didn't know how to go about missionary work in Iraq.

Days were starting to pass at a faster pace and work direction changed. A corporate decision was made to crate components up for sending to Saudi Arabia for rebuilding. Since wood is scarce in Iraq, how were we supposed to crate things up? It was one more example of the detachment from reality that stateside management had about our conditions and abilities. I actually believe they thought we could go down to Home Depot, pop out the corporate credit card, and get what we needed. Our site leader Brent was frustrated. Trying to please the upper levels and explain reality must have been an awesome chore. But supplies were scrounged, and the task was accomplished, despite resembling a fire drill. New technical help had arrived with men from Scotland, Ireland, and the Philippines. With new help onboard, we could split up the tasks, and they would help supervise. There were still replacement parts in limbo from Italy and the US that were getting held up in Kuwaiti and Saudi customs. But with new help to subdivide the workers, we could begin other work. Our outbound crates sat there at the plant ready to be shipped out.

An additional frustration was a huge machine shop error on the large rotating shaft. This monster component had to go back to be reworked in Saudi Arabia also. It was basically embarrassing. But the Iraqi men were accepting and understanding. I think it surprised them that we would allow such an oversight to get by us. But it demonstrated to them that we were not infallible and that we were competent to find our mistakes, admit them, and correct them promptly. So, progress was being made, but in different directions than originally planned. I was yet unaware, but while the pace of activity increased, I was about to be introduced to the month of Ramadan.

Without going into the history and concept behind the practice of Ramadan, it is basically considered a month of fasting. It's based on a lunar calendar which means the dates of observance change over time, but when I was there it lasted from roughly mid-October to mid-November. It is a sacred commemoration practiced throughout all Islamic societies. The rules are not consistent with Christian or Latter-day Saint practice of a fast. From sunrise to sunset, no food or drink is taken. All the guys in the crew who smoked cigarettes gave them up. There is an eating period in the evening after sunset when families break the fast and socialize. According to colleagues familiar with the Middle East, some sectors of Islamic society will stay up late eating and socializing until well after midnight throughout the period. The result on the industrial activity in the region is that some of it suffers. We were asked by plant management not to smoke, eat, or drink in front of any of the workers during the Ramadan period. It was still quite hot and the lack of water throughout the day seemed harsh and could stagnate productivity. To get decent work out of the guys until around lunch was not a problem. After lunch, it was a wash. Men would go into some little corner and lay out a mat and nap. I wasn't enthusiastic about a tough afternoon of work either. It was still hot and going without water throughout the day seemed unrealistic. So, I concentrated on parts inventory and drank water and ate lunch in secret as my work crew suffered through the day. To me, it compared somewhat to that week between Christmas and New Year's in the US, except there were four weeks of it. You go to work, but you're not into it. And you just go due to the obligation, but you really bide your time until after the New Year.

Malik's father died unexpectedly, and he was out for a few days. When he returned, he took time and explained to us his responsibilities for the funeral. It was interesting to learn that there was a time limit to prepare the body and perform the burial. The dead are buried in daylight hours, but throughout the night, Malik had to continually read from the Koran to his father's corpse while the body was ceremonially prepared for burial the next day. I found it interesting to note how Malik didn't mind discussing with us such a personal experience, and again, it seemed like he was doing missionary work for our benefit. But being the spiritual man that he is, I believe he wanted to share the cultural and spiritual aspect of this experience as a courtesy to us.

So, progress picked up and then progress lost ground. Things got exciting in the evening on the Coalition base as some elements mobilized to support the US forces as the Fallujah assault began. We had the additional technical people at work for over a couple of weeks now, but the month of Ramadan cut productivity to a certain extent. But there was more to the story than blaming Ramadan. Our outbound crates still sat there at the plant, ready to be shipped out. Three weeks would pass before the components would get shipped from our location. We found out later there were other replacement parts bound for our project, but they were never shipped out from the place of origin. To blame the month of Ramadan wasn't entirely fair, but I heard the grumbling starting from people at corporate. The original schedule was being exceeded by weeks at this point, and a corporate decision was made to decrease the technical staff. I ended up staying in Iraq along with four others, including Brent. Our Irishman and one of the Filipinos would have to leave. It was odd to explain to the plant guys where their supervision had gone after only about three weeks of time. I believe they felt bad because of the danger that faced us working in Iraq and the difficulty of keeping people there. But we settled back into the change within a day or so.

Everyone adjusted and we had gotten into the routine again for a few days. Getting up and leaving the base for the ride to work had gotten routine again. It was a Sunday morning, and we were scheduled for a late-morning departure. Our sister site security team and contractors had just left the camp compound, headed for the gate and their worksite. I was gathering my gear in my room when a huge concussion rocked the entire camp. The natural reaction is to immediately look at your watch. Coalition forces ordinance disposal teams would routinely detonate on the hour or half hour, but this explosion was off by ten minutes. There was some commotion in camp as people scrambled around and some of us looked for our security men to verify that we weren't under mortar attack. Then all the two-way radios started going off with "Contact! Contact! Call sign Tango Three has contact!" Our sister team was returned to camp promptly, and one of the engineers told us a roadside bomb had gone off a short distance outside the Coalition gate. We had one security team out that morning returning from a personnel transfer assignment. It was one of their vehicles that was hit by the roadside bomb. Two of the three security men in that vehicle were confirmed dead. The delicate balance between safety and death had been tipped.

CHAPTER 8

Two men were now dead that I had been walking and talking with just the day or two before. It was a solemn thought to imagine the shock and grief suffered by the loved ones back in their home countries. One was from England, and the other was a South African. They were good men. The UK man had been assigned to our security crew for a few days a week or so before. I remember him in the workshop guarding me one day and the plant guys thought he was not as cheerful as he could have been. I explained that he was probably tired of being away from home and was looking forward to some much-needed time off that he was scheduled for. The South African man was never assigned to our crew, but he and I would see each other in camp and give cordial greetings as we would cross paths.

The deaths missed the major media circuit back in the US and Britain as far as we could tell. The status of our safety was being discussed at a corporate level and chances were that we would be removed from Iraq until a new security strategy was implemented. Questions were being raised regarding the level of response from some of the Coalition forces following the attack. A military patrol drove right past the downed vehicle immediately after the explosion. Additionally, a smaller contingent of the Coalition forces were recently assigned the task of bomb sweeping the area each morning. There was a rumor going around that this patrol didn't possess the sophisticated Electronic Counter Measures (ECM) equipment such as the larger British and American patrols had, and this caused them to be a little less efficient in their sweeps. ECM is a radio-jamming device that disrupts any radio signals that could be used to detonate a bomb within a certain area. Two-way radios and cell phones are methods used for roadside bomb detonation. It would be sad if there were any truth to that rumor, but we never found out either way.

Many locals worked on the base, and the front gate was always crowded with people coming and going. Closer to the base access road and the main road, there would always be locals outside of parked cars rummaging around the old military vehicle carcasses and the trash. Most of the debris was left there from the Saddam regime and had never been cleaned up. There were acres of junk, and it looked as if new trash was put out there on a regular basis. People were always snooping through it. Some days it looked as if families were out there having a picnic or taking a break from a long drive. They would park their beat-up vehicles right off the road and next to the trash and wander around.

Our security team continually commented about the amount of activity that was allowed to take place so close to the front gate. There was fear that insurgents were using the area for surveillance on troops and our movements in and out of the gate. We were always alert for any type of nicer-looking vehicles parked outside. Anything other than the usual, well-worn, older Toyota Land Cruiser or Datsun mini pickups with the standard broken windshield was suspect. Several times, we noticed a late model vehicle parked off to the side with the hood propped up while Western-dressed men stood around as if something mechanical was wrong. Within the course of the day, the military patrols would chase these men off, but after a few days passed, there would be others.

As the corporate decision makers discussed our fate, there was some pressure on us to decide our status in Iraq, and whether we would stay and continue our work or leave for security reasons. To me, this choice seemed unfair. I wanted to know the response strategy first, then decide based on that knowledge. It's possible that corporate authorities needed to know who wanted to leave first, so they could then make a security plan based on those remaining. Looking back, that seems fair enough from their position. But what I wanted to know was what were they going to do for us to make staying in Iraq more palatable? All the Filipino workers wanted to go home, and most had been in Iraq awhile by this time. The decision was made to evacuate to Kuwait by convoy while corporate, security, and military authorities discussed cooperative measures to allow a safe return.

After having been in Iraq for almost nine weeks, we were going to Kuwait for an indefinite period while things settled down. Once again, it was an absolutely quiet ride all the way to the border. This time around, the Coalition forces escort possessed ECM equipment, which settled some nerves during the trip. Our belongings were with us in case we ended up leaving for home. After safe arrival into Kuwait, we were checked in to a nice hotel in Kuwait City and started to remember what life was about. Glamorous spreads of food and desserts three times a day or more if desired, along with shopping trips, movies, and decent phone connections back home once again. Each of the Filipinos made their flights back to Manila within a day. Being the good husband that I am, I left out the part about our two security men being killed by a roadside bomb when explaining the Kuwait trip to family back home. So, we enjoyed the feasting and shopping and continued walking for exercise in the evenings.

I got to discuss more about the region with some of our local security contractors and corporate people that were communicating with us daily. This unexpected vacation break allowed me the time to learn more about the Middle East and its people. Central to recent Kuwait history was the Iraqi invasion of 1990. It was a traumatic event for Kuwaitis, and there are many historical accounts describing the brutality of the Iraqi occupation of Kuwait. Americans may be aware of the oil fires set by retreating Iraqi forces at hundreds of oil wells, but the inhumane actions of the occupying forces might not be as common knowledge to the West as it is to the Kuwaitis.

To this day, they are still grateful to the US and its allies for the liberation that followed. More than just allowing for US troops to be stationed there, private signs and flags on public display still openly thank US troops for their sacrifice. They celebrate Kuwait Liberation Day on February 26, which marks the end of Iraqi aggression in 1991. It is a long holiday coinciding with February 25 as Kuwait National Day, which marks independence from Britain in 1961.

Beyond the flags and signs of support, I saw more evidence that Kuwaitis are tolerant of other cultures and religions within their shores. A large Catholic population of mostly expatriates reside there. In 1945, a Carmelite mission priest from Basra, Iraq, ventured down to Kuwait to check on his members and establish a cathedral for worship. At that time, non-Kuwaitis were not allowed to purchase land, so a prominent Kuwaiti Sheikh donated the land for the building of the cathedral. The official Kuwaiti Catholic website even lists Latter-day Saints as worshipping within the tiny desert nation. One characteristic in this prosperous nation's Islamic culture greatly impressed me, and that is tolerance. Even though Kuwait is not purely democratic, the people enjoy liberty and express a tolerant attitude. As a nation they have respect and tolerance towards others.

The United Arab Emirates is another example of liberty found in a country that is not a pure democracy. Sheikh Zayed Bin Sultan Al Nahyan, president of the United Arab Emirates, passed away in early November 2004. The Iraqi workers made mention of this to me while we were at work the day after his death, and even they were somewhat somber that day. The Kuwaiti papers were still publishing editorials extolling the virtues of this man while we were in Kuwait. I'm not sure if the significance of his life and its effect on the region was passed on to the American press. But the biggest contrast today between UAE and Iraq is in the lifestyle of the citizens. Dubai in the

United Arab Emirates is one of the world's great cities and even has a Latter-day Saint ward listed on the Church website. The Sheikh came to power in the mid-sixties, compared to Saddam in the early seventies. The difference between these two nations couldn't be more extreme. One leader was a tyrant who scalped the nation of its natural resources for personal and military gain for decades, while the other used the country's wealth for commercial enterprise development, technological infrastructure advancement, and philanthropic humanitarian aid. It's true that the Emirate leader also enjoyed luxurious palaces with elaborate settings. But the difference between the two countries in terms of the citizens, the freedoms, and the commerce is remarkable. Yes, the UAE surely has some typical struggles as any society does. Look carefully, and you might find some of your clothes "Made in UAE." However, Iraq fared differently. Even Malik told me his first job after college was mandatory work in the engineering department of an Iraqi government missile design complex. It all just demonstrated to me where the focus was for Saddam's Iraq. What a shame.

Kuwait is still a strict society that does not tolerate alcohol and drugs, and sexual promiscuity is not part of the culture. Muslim women cover themselves, and the Kuwaiti women have only recently been awarded voting status. However, there are no "morality police," such as in Saudi Arabia, who patrol and apprehend offenders of Islamic law. While I never felt threatened in Kuwait, there was a difference. A majority of the time I couldn't even get eye contact in the hotel hallway with Kuwaiti men as we crossed paths. It occurred to me that maybe our modern, Western values have stereotyped us to a point of disdain. This was a far cry from the well-wishers in Iraq waving, smiling, shaking hands, and grateful to see us there to help. But the gratitude from Kuwait for Western help is still there, and many times I felt that the freedom and tolerance of their society is the fruits of our labor.

Decisions were made to enhance our safety in Iraq, and we were mobilized back to the camp on the Coalition base. The whole episode lasted about fourteen days with ten of those days spent in Kuwait. Arriving back at the plant after being absent, we faced a similar reaction to what had happened after the roadside bomb incident weeks earlier. Many of the Iraqis were trying to figure out if they remembered the deceased men. There was heated discussion among themselves and then gracious thanks for our work to this point along with prayers in our behalf. Mohammad got into detail about this with me this time. He wanted to know if there was anything the guys could do to help or if his men could guard us for safety. Kind of like the "safe house" concept. He was offering that we stay at the plant or in their homes if necessary for our protection, and his men could take turns guarding us. Sometimes people offer assistance or solutions in the form of idle talk, not really intending to carry through. But these men were serious and were in discussion on how to do this. Of course, the answer was "no way," but I carefully explained to Mohammad that I didn't think our security contractor would allow that. The sincerity of the gesture overwhelmed me, and I had to try to smile about it as a response while at the same time trying to avoid my eyes from welling up in tears. Once again, I received genuine concern and honest gratitude from the Iraqi plant workers. A bond had formed that I just can't express in words.

We were nearing the end of project funding, the month of Ramadan was over, daytime temperatures had dropped, and Christmas season was getting close. Our large rotating shaft was corrected and delivered, and we were working toward installing it as soon as possible. The refurbished components had shipped, and we expected these materials to arrive any day and productivity to increase. Work pace picked up, and everyone was busy. I needed my Arabic-English phrasebook and realized I had left it in the workshop before we were rushed off to Kuwait. Not surprisingly, it was stowed away carefully to avoid Alibaba. The guys had been taking turns studying it while we were gone. They were working to improve their English, so they could better communicate with me. Once again, I found myself deeply touched by another thoughtful gesture on their part—sharpening their language skills for all to benefit.

I was trying to maximize the work effort when Adnan hurt his back while lifting some heavy items. When I asked about his condition, the guys confided in me that the local Iraqi medical facilities are "*moo-rah-ha*" (no good). They asked if I could get medicine for them. Thinking a little malingering might be going on, I purchased some ibuprofen that evening at the base and gave it to Adnan the next day. It never occurred to me what medicines they had access to. Adnan was back at work on reduced duty the day after and sincerely thankful for my assistance. He was somewhat astonished at the effectiveness of these fat pills I gave him to swallow. I, too, was surprised at what a reaction to this simple medication he had.

This got me thinking that they didn't have the personal funds for ibuprofen if they were required to purchase it. Or maybe they didn't have access to the medicine at the hospital or clinic. Perhaps the medical professionals didn't have the expertise to recommend or prescribe it, or the quality was so poor that the medicines were ineffective. Either way, it caused some concern to me, so I did a little web research the following evening and what I found was disturbing. There were several websites with personal accounts of religious and humanitarian leadership visits to Iraqi facilities throughout the country. Issues concerning medical equipment purchases and UN sanctions were detailed. Suffice it to say that the guys at the plant were giving me the straight scoop. The Iraqi medical industry is "moo-rah-ha." It would be interesting to see some straight investigative reporting on the structure behind the Iraqi medical system as it was and where it was headed.

It wasn't just the medical supplies that seemed to be difficult to obtain. As we had learned before, trying to obtain basic industrial tooling and supplies was difficult and not everything was available. One of the workers I recognized came up to me with two other men I hadn't seen before. Galib, Malik, Mohammad, and the other English speakers were not with them. Somewhat frantically, they approached and handed me an empty can of Isomil One baby formula made by Abbott Laboratories in powder form. It was labeled in English and Arabic. We worked through the language barrier as usual, and they asked if I could obtain this in Kuwait or Jordan for them and how many days it would take. My guess was about three days or more, so I held up three fingers while shaking my head yes. They explained that the baby was extremely sick and wouldn't take other formulas. The apparent father offered me money, asking for two cans, but I declined for the moment. I explained that it might not be available, but I wasn't sure if they understood.

Still, I took these men seriously and fired off an email to our purchasing contact in Kuwait asking for the unusual items. To add a little begging to the request, I explained in the email that the men up here have never taken advantage of me, there was some urgency in their tone, and if a side trip to a Kuwait supermarket on personal time would be all right. He agreed and said he had the personal funds to cover. I included a digital photo of the can and assured him I would pay him back with cash on my way back home through Kuwait sometime before Christmas. A few hours later I saw Galib and asked him about this unusual request. He seemed to know all about it. He said it wasn't available in Iraq. "What about Baghdad?" I asked, and he said no. We had a new tool room attendant that seemed to have a grip on the local market goods, so I asked him to check in the local market. I guess I still thought these other men just didn't do a good job looking around for this brand. "*Muffie-mushkilla*," which means "no problem," was his reply, and I gave him the empty can. He came back the day after and said he couldn't find any. Luckily, our Kuwaiti contact was more than glad to help, and he had purchased two cans the same day the email came through. He dropped them off at our security contractor's Kuwait office right away, and the goods were waiting for transport to our project on the next run.

So, the three days came and went. I asked our security men if they had done border runs recently or air freight pick up in Baghdad and if they saw any baby food come through. Nobody knew anything. Finally, after five days, I went into the camp security manager's office that evening about to ask about it. This man was a great gentleman, spoke perfect Queen's English, and was always anxious to help. He always concerned himself about our morale in addition to our overall safety in Iraq. My two cans of Isomil One were stacked on his desk. He thought it was muscle-building powder that some of his security team guys had ordered and didn't pick up yet. We both had a quick chuckle, then I grabbed the cans to bring to work the next morning.

When I handed the cans over to the tool room attendant first thing in the morning, he took off immediately. Before long the baby's father and a small contingent of other men I had never seen before found me and expressed total gratitude. There was plenty of handshakes and bowing of heads with the follow-up of hands placed over the heart from all in this group as they crowded around me. Later I found out they were houseguests of Galib from Hilla.

It was times like this where I wished for a devoted Arabic interpreter. The bits and pieces of communication were difficult, and chasing down Malik for everything would have demanded too much of him. I tried to get the whole baby food story, but as usual, it was tough. Somehow the parents discovered the baby would only take the Isomil One formula. This baby was very sick now, and they only had a few cans of the formula left. The intent of the father's trip to see Galib was to get more baby food.

Having our tool room attendant search through the local markets didn't locate the particular brand they needed in their case. And there might not have been a large choice of baby foods to choose from locally, if any, because baby food was on the UN sanctions list. This shocked me. What's baby food doing on the UN sanctions list? If that's the case, then Iraqis have most likely been using a black-market economy for these critical needs for years, or just plain doing without. It will probably still take time for market forces to line up and supply quality goods to the population since the UN sanctions were lifted in May 2003. Here I was, over a year after sanctions were lifted, and items as critical as baby formula were still difficult to obtain. I was glad to assist and couldn't accept their money when I gave them the cans. Something about helping the truly needy and then taking money for it just negates the whole experience.

As I honestly explained in my email to Kuwait, these men never took advantage of me. I have been to other impoverished areas in the world where people would clamor around and ask for things. So far ibuprofen, proper tooling, and now some baby food were the only requests that came from them. By this time, the sharing nature of these people was so evident to me. Every day was an open invitation to eat lunch in the shop with the guys and they always supplied the food. They would start asking me about mid-morning if I would come to the shop for lunch. They just craved the cultural exchange and loved it when I would sit down with them and eat. If I didn't eat with them for a few days, they'd bring us some home-cooked goods or would purchase these very simple, honey-covered pastries from a local bakery to give to us to eat. Stinginess wasn't part of their character, and they shared what they had despite their income levels.

There was one humorous circumstance we had in regard to the amount of hand cleaner available for the job. We had several large tubs of it sent with the tooling kit, and a couple of small 16 oz. containers that were getting used up quickly. I had grabbed one of the small containers and found a little hiding place for it in the washbasin area. After getting dirty working with the guys on the equipment, I'd run back there and wash up with my stash, then put it back in the hidden place. Every so often Mohammad would come back there with me, I'd break out the goods, and we'd wash up. One time, we both went to the washbasin, and I couldn't find the container. I had kicked it too far into its secret place and had to lift up the large grating to grab it.

Mohammad looked at me with a broad smile and said, "All the guys know it's under there." He told me that the guys made sure nobody was using it and periodically checked that it was there in its proper place. I had to chuckle. It was so much in their character to always be aware of the things that helped me and the other engineers throughout the day and make sure we had what we needed at our fingertips. Just like Ahmed, so willing to help regardless of how menial the chore seemed to be.

The next major milestone for us was installing the large rotating shaft, which was several tons in weight and represented a significant portion of the work scope. This was a critical task and required cooperation from all workers involved, otherwise it could be chaotic and a safety hazard. The guys banded together, and we worked fervently to prepare for installation of this large component as quickly as possible. Doing this is stressful anywhere in the world. Despite not being highly experienced in this specific task, the guys pulled together in a coordinated fashion, and we got it done promptly and correctly, while keeping the chaos factor to a minimum. There was a complete sense of accomplishment after this. I believe calls for a feast were being uttered throughout the plant floor. I did some high-fives with all the guys, and they were amused at the custom. Eventually, I caught them doing a few high-fives with each other. It was impressive to be a part of the unity that was taking place. I'd like to think of the increased efforts as a response to the guys enjoying the workday.

Despite our recent successes, there was still pressure behind the scenes from corporate people to move up the schedule, which added tension to the project. Additionally, an incomplete finish was in sight due to funding exhaustion. Management was negotiating for extensions and additional funding, while US government representatives were asking for firm dollar pricing to complete the project. Many communications were taking place in response to the incomplete work scope compared to the submitted schedule. We were questioned as to why we were so off the original schedule. The reason was that the work progress and the schedule didn't match up and were unrealistic. Replacement parts, shipping logistics, and particulars dealing with skill levels and tooling all had a play in the pace. Brent was getting pressured from above, which disengaged him from the actual work. Malik had taught us the Arabic expression "*ta-del-el*," which meant "it will be alright" or "it will measure up." I heard him use that expression in frustration with Brent many more times in frequency as we chugged along closer to the end of these last few weeks. It got to the point where I was using that phrase with Brent a few times myself. But more frustration was yet to come.

One morning as I went out to find the guys and greet them, I was met by a less than enthusiastic crowd. Mohammad told me there was some kind of report that was not good, and all the guys were discouraged. This was a morale breaker for the guys, especially after an outstanding performance installing the critical rotating shaft. Their jubilant attitude was gone. It was such an attitude change from what I had been working with all this time that I went looking for Malik right away to get clarification. It turned out that Brent had submitted an official report to corporate folks and predominantly blamed the labor for the delays to this point. I never saw this report, but somehow the workers learned about it.

According to Mohammad and Malik, there was no mention of the shipping delays, the incorrect parts that were supplied, or other issues that caused problems. When Malik explained how the guys felt, I went into human damage-control mode. On this issue, I had to divorce myself from Brent in front of the guys and then go confront him privately. That ended up being a waste of energy, as I never got any info out of him. Actually, I felt bad for him. He was rather young to be carrying the great weight of contract failure. It's likely that Brent told corporate the facts, and it was spun to their advantage before being put back out to the client. Regardless, the guys saw the origin as coming from Brent, and they were upset.

A sad commentary resulted from this event. Al, the local Iraqi man and US government rep for the job, had come out to the site to check progress and gather details. As I tried to defend the guys' work and how I felt about the delays, Al interrupted me. He impassionedly told me that during Saddam's rule they lost many engineers. Many fled and some were killed, so Al explained that many of them would lie to save their lives. Then he said, "But it is sad to see that your people lie to make money for their companies. I see a big difference in this." After that exchange of words, it was difficult for me to say anything in return. Our sister site project was experiencing similar tones regarding schedule delay, and my Scottish counterpart was being upfront and honest in his overall assessment. Al wanted me to know he appreciated the honesty and defense of the work crew at both sites, despite the blame episodes that were taking place behind the scenes. We all felt badly about this whole situation.

So, I worked on regaining the guys' confidence. After three days of once again struggling through the limited communication, trying to relay positive encouragement to the guys individually and collectively, we got back on track. Something else was going on that everyone noticed by this time. I was getting burned out. I'd gone over ninety days without a break except for the Kuwait stay, and I began to make mistakes. The guys started quizzing me to make sure I was okay. They knew I didn't drink, but they began asking me to make sure I hadn't broken my standards the night before. Several critical components were installed wrong, and I let it go. When the guys took their breaks, they'd discuss things they didn't feel good about. Then, one of them would come over to point it out to me, but he'd do it in the form of a question. They conducted themselves in a most respectful manner, always giving me an avenue to save face. It would have been easy and justified for them to confront me and let me know how stupid I was. My job was mechanical assembly, and at this critical time, this is what I was getting paid for. With morale recovery from the report incident still recent history, the guys could have exacted some revenge. But just the opposite happened on all these occasions. Instead, they used the events to teach me another Arabic phrase, "*moo-ma-coo*," which means "mind gone" or "no brain." They all chipped in with extra-watchful eyes to make sure nothing critical was amiss. In essence, they covered for me. We were working with smiling faces and enthusiasm again. It was a true teamwork project.

The weather had suddenly changed a week or so before, and we were all wearing light jackets and gloves throughout the day now. Several hard rainstorms blasted down on the countryside during this period, and we actually had to contend with some humidity along with very chilly mornings. Daylight was also noticeably shorter, so we had to adjust our arrival and departure times to compensate, which made for a shorter workday.

One evening, our security team took a different route to save time, and we ended up lost. We drove through several small farms that evening, turning around, then turning around again, trying to get our bearings straight. At one point a local land-owner wearing full traditional Arab clothing and headgear came out of his house and tried to intercept us. Our vehicles scrambled to turn around and get off his property. I looked back and saw he was holding his hand up in the air, motioning for us to come to him. As he watched us frantically making our exit, he pointed his finger in the direction of the proper exit. He wanted to help us, but we were too nervous.

But the incident revealed more than a willingness of the locals to provide some assistance to a bunch of lost armored vehicles in the Iraqi desert at sunset. The man wasn't scared of us. He didn't come out with an AK-47 to push us off his property. He came out unarmed to offer help, knowing full well we would have been armed to the teeth whether we were military or private security teams. This man was the typical local who would be working the fields while his children would run up to wave and give us the thumbs-up. It was obvious who was scared and who wasn't. I hoped it wouldn't be long until both sides had no apprehension about the other and the word "contact" does not necessarily signify a negative event.

The next day I took a large whiteboard out of our office trailer and fastened it to the wall in the guys' workshop. Mohammad and I would go over the daily work expected and write it on the board for all to see. He would translate to the guys and keep track of progress. We were getting into the fine details of final assembly. Omar, the engineer from the other crew, surprised me regarding the dry-erase board. For all his good English skills, his refined knowledge of machinery, and his educated disposition and stature, I don't think he'd ever seen a dry-erase board before. I couldn't recall seeing any kind of chalkboards or even a bulletin board in the power plant section. His request to me was if I could get a smaller one for him to use at home, and he would reimburse me. He wanted one to keep track of chores for his children. I gave him a sly answer of no, saying, "Because your wife will use it to write down chores for you." Even with his superior English, I had to select my words carefully to ensure he had the meaning correct. But he understood immediately, and we both had a good laugh. In Arabic, he told the guys who were nearby what I just said. I didn't want to embarrass him by asking if he'd never seen a dry-erase board before. Rather than pursuing my curiosity, I told him I'd try to purchase one for him.

Our time in Iraq was drawing to a close, and it was now becoming evident to us that our job would not be completed before I left. I don't think the guys were thinking along those lines at this point. They were immersed in the work and keeping pace to achieve completion.

At a specific moment, it really hit me hard when I realized that I honestly would miss these men when I left. I looked at Ayad on a particular morning and said to him, "I'm going to miss you." He didn't understand what I meant. Their smiles, gracious greetings and offerings, and genuine concern for us are features not always found in our Western societies. When I sat down with them for lunch that day, I decided to take the bull by the horns and ask them some probing questions that were at the forefront of the political discussion in the US and UK.

I was interested in the question of weapons of mass destruction first. Did they know anything? What did they think? The response came immediately. Basically, they said to me, "You are America. Why do you have to have anything threatening to you before you will help us? Saddam was bad, period, and wasn't that enough to come to Iraq's aid?" Who else would help them? they wondered. They said, "You (America) are blessed by God. Why would you not help us?" The bottom line was that any bad thing was possible with Saddam as their leader.

And they shared with me how they felt about the ordinary Iraqi citizen. They explained that, as a whole, Iraqis are good people who have been oppressed for too long. Yes, there are bad people mixed in like anywhere else. And these bad people have access to deadly weapons. But the good are a silent majority who quietly go about their lives. Galib had told me in the past that Baghdad was full of good people too. And that every time a car bomb would go off, the crowd would gather and offer help. The dialogue got me thinking about the mindset of a suicide bomber. What did they think they were accomplishing by forfeiting their lives? If secret combinations can persuade individuals to forfeit their life for evil, isn't it only logical that freedom-loving nations have individuals willing to forfeit their life if necessary for good? I started to look at our military men and women as active wheat, working to contain the tares.

The whole exchange forced me to reflect back on the self-serving attitude of "Why should I care?" that some people have. Why not just sit back and enjoy my life and be oblivious to others and their plight? I was hoping the guys didn't know there was a vocal movement against the Iraq invasion in the US, and I didn't want to be confronted about it. How do you explain about people that aren't willing to help? Does the West, with all its blessings and prosperity, still have compassion as the foundation of our societies? And what does the gospel teach in regard to this? Is it only individuals we help and not nations? It would have been tough to explain any of this. But the guys didn't ask. Perhaps they knew but were polite for my sake. Knowing their character, that was probably the case.

I asked them about Iran. Is that what they wanted? Iranian support? And the answer was a resounding no. They wanted free access to Iranian holy sites, and they wanted Iranians to have access to Iraqi holy sites, but that was it. From their perspective, why would they want a theocratic government and Islamic law ruling them? Their leader was Ali al-Sistani, and that's where they get their guidance from on spiritual matters. They considered him a good man, and they talked highly of him. They didn't want an entire government involved in issues of Islamic law. Employment security and disposable income were the critical issues to them. And I realized they were just like us. They want to work hard and succeed and use the fruits of their labors to better their life. Satisfaction could be the ability to go down to the market and buy a new rug for the front doorstep or modernize their homes with computers and other appliances. It is the simple things of life and acceptance into the modern world economy they crave.

That whole exchange troubled me when I thought of the extent that some of my countrymen were past feeling. I wondered how long it would be before self-interest and self-ishness completely defined us as a nation. "You (America) are blessed by God, why would you *not* help us?" That question just kept going through my mind for several days. I couldn't help but think that we live in the greatest country in the world, and where much is given, much is required.

Malik gave me a bit of a scare early the next afternoon. The men had just said their prayers and ate lunch. He came over to our office trailer and asked for Brent and me to accompany him to the workshop. I didn't have a clue what this was about, but I figured that perhaps the guys might have some kind of concerns or complaints about the vigorous work pace and wanted some discussion. Or maybe my "weapons of mass destruction" and Iranian discussions were too invasive, and I was in trouble. The bad report incident wasn't that long ago and maybe it wasn't forgotten entirely as I had thought. Quietly, we walked into the workshop where about fifteen or so of the plant men were crowded around. As we stepped up to the table, we saw a large, round cake with a candle in the middle. It was Brent's birthday, and the men had gotten together and purchased a cake for him at a local bakery. Solemn faces turned to smiles as we broke our stern facial expressions and everyone started yelling "Happy birthday" in English and Arabic. We sat down and cut up the rough-looking cake. The dark, thick sugary frosting wasn't near to the quality we were accustomed to back home. We dished out the cake slices on paper hand rags from the tool bins, and I just marveled at the entire situation and the congenial manner of these Iraqi men.

The contractors working onsite regretted the early departure. Along with the stress of homesickness, we had the burden of failing to get more power to the populace before we departed. Behind the scenes, the US government representative had lost faith in our ability to complete the assignment, and negotiations for us to continue ceased. We were now scheduling ourselves for what remaining work could be accomplished before our departure. To complicate matters, there was a discretionary mechanical measurement of internal components that was determined to be out of tolerance. Upon closer scrutiny of the detailed machinery drawing, there was a conflict between me and those back at the corporate level as to the proper interpretation of this drawing detail. My Scottish counterpart from the sister site had strong feelings about this issue as well. After much discussion, both of us realized that we were correct and corporate folks just wouldn't listen. We had to allow them to prevail and extend the work scope within the limited remaining timeframe.

For Mohammad and the guys, this incident taught them a lesson in attention to detail and the importance of procedural checks. They were not aware of the internal disagreement we had among ourselves. They only knew that they went through extra work to assure that the equipment was being reassembled correctly. In the process, Mohammad learned that critical steps shouldn't be bypassed just to complete a task; changes in plans and extra measures can be necessary. This was good training in attention to detail by example. And Mohammad started to scrutinize the assembly drawings in greater detail at this point, directing the guys to make checks in areas I wasn't concerned about.

Although no announcements had been made, we were all now aware that my final day was closing in, as it was for the rest of the contractor team. Because of security protocols, I couldn't tell everyone my exact departure date. But the guys started doing things for me and the rest of the team as send-off gifts and well-wishing. Adding some comfort to these final couple of weeks, our security team was rotated, and this new team was entirely South African nationals. For whatever reason, the South African men tended to have a pleasing ambiance about them that radiated wherever they were. They smiled more, enjoyed engaging in small talk and discussion with the plant workers, and had courteous driving characteristics throughout the towns and countryside as well as inside the plant. Apparently tattoos and body piercing are not popular with South African men, so along with their pleasant character was a clean appearance that set a relaxed tone. Even the Iraqi guys commented to me several times that these were good men.

My favorite characteristic of the South African men was their willingness to allow us to throw food and candies out to the waving children during our trips back to the base in the evenings. Every lunch there were plenty of extra apples, oranges, and potato chips from our bag lunches that would pile up on one of the worktables in the office trailer. The bags of potato chips we would gather up and usually give to Galib for his daughter. We would collect the fruit into a single bag and direct our security men to "perform the mission."

On several sections of our travel routes, the dirt roads would wind around large concrete barriers and earthen walls.

Local children from the surrounding homes and farms always ran up close to the road to look, wave, and give the thumbs-up sign. Taking precautions not to entice the children too close to the moving vehicles, the security men would use the last vehicle as the drop vehicle. They would slow down to an absolute crawl, then crack the front passenger door for a hefty toss of the bag outward and toward the rear of the vehicle. We expanded this little operation to include candy we would purchase from the base post exchange in the evenings.

Before long, one could find several of us contractors up at the post exchange in the evening buying goodies for what we titled, "Operation Candy Drop." The smiles and waves we would see as we looked rearward were priceless as the children would crowd around the dropped goods and start to dig in and divvy up. Since these little activities were against security rules, this was our secret between us and our South African security team while back in camp. If any of the UK guys were with us for a day or two, Operation Candy Drop was suspended.

Galib decided to have his wife fix us a big spread for lunch within the last few days before we left. As he brought everything into the office trailer that afternoon, along came his nine-year-old daughter to help. The pronunciation of her name had a guttural sound associated with it that I just plain couldn't do. Galib worked with me on this until he finally gave up. This cute little girl came in wearing modern-looking blue jeans with some hand embroidery on them and a very conservative button blouse with a light jacket. Everything she was wearing seemed to be in fashion even by Western standards. I believe Galib's wife was involved with some kind of school teaching, so she wasn't available to come meet us and assist. After the assortment of Iraqi bread, a dark rice dish with nuts and spices, and two different styles of grilled or roasted chicken was spread out, the little girl sat down next to her dad and stared relentlessly at me and some of the others enjoying our lunch. We took the opportunity to shower her with different candies we had stashed in the trailer to break up her fixation on us. Everyone anxiously watched her reaction. As any little girl would do, she dove right into them as soon as Dad gave the go-ahead signal. It seemed that she liked the Tootsie Pops the best. None of these candies were available in the local Iraqi market to our knowledge.

I watched closely how Galib handled his daughter as she rendered assistance with serving our lunch. Just as any father would do, he was firm and a little gruff as he gave her directions. But also, just as any father would do, he displayed his love for her as she sat next to him, and he stroked her beautiful long brown hair and laid his arm around her shoulder. The sight of a father who loves his little girl requires no spoken language for the interpretation to be rendered. And the same for a little girl's comfort of Dad being there next to her in the presence of strange men from the other side of the world. These are universal feelings that are not subject to cultural boundaries. Despite the focus on sons in their culture, I learned from those I met that these Muslim fathers were in no way less inclined to their daughters.

Tariq "Two Wives" had talked with me many times throughout the project about the native dried dates that were available from the local market, and he had promised to deliver a large sack for me to take home. Not being a big fan of dates, I politely held my tongue and accepted the offer. The only experience I had with dates goes back to my toddler days. My mother bought a package or two of a messy, compressed block of dates that required a thorough hand washing after eating. But Tariq finally came through and brought me the goods. It was a tightly pressed brick of the most delicious dates I have ever tasted. Crudely wrapped in hand-cut cellophane wrapping, these were dry dates compressed together with sesame seeds throughout. Kind of a natural candy with a tinge of the sesame seed flavor. Hand washing was not required after pulling them off the brick and putting them into your mouth. Tariq explained that this type of date used to be reserved for royalty and gifts to dignitaries since ancient times. But during the Saddam years, they were scarce because of the demand the government would put on them. Only recently had they become somewhat available in the local market. I was honored that Tariq would spend his hard-earned money on such a surprisingly pleasant gift for me. They were so good that I had a difficult time trying to save the bulk of them to take home.

My departure day finally arrived. For security reasons, I still couldn't tell the guys that this was my last day until late in the afternoon. I was scheduled to return to Iraq and finish the job after a short Christmas break with my family in Virginia, but all the details had to be kept secret. We were having a normal workday, and everyone was on a roll with their assignments. I ate a quick lunch in the office, then came over to visit the guys while they were still chatting. They had just finished having said their prayers and eaten their lunch. It was a tremendous mixing of emotions for me, but the notion of coming back after Christmas and the men's excitement over the upcoming Iraqi elections was so comforting that leaving wasn't as painful as it could have been.

The dry-erase board had been neglected for about one day, so I updated it with Mohammad and told him I was leaving in an hour or so and wouldn't be back until after the holidays. I updated the white board with pending work items and left a goodbye note for one of the guys that had stayed home that day. Mohammad immediately went out and spread the word. Galib didn't know what was going on, walked into the shop during this, and started to read the whiteboard. He was distraught and walked outside after giving me a bear hug. He was tearing up and didn't want me to see. I went back to the office trailer and gathered up some personal items to give out to the guys. There was still the matter of my two Arabic copies of the Book of Mormon. I wanted to leave them behind somehow. Not knowing the exact procedure that would be appropriate to do this, I coaxed Galib and Chalupe into the trailer and just held up the books while raising my eyebrows—a somewhat universal language for "Do you want this?" Galib had been interested all along since he had read several chapters of Ether. Chalupe was honored to receive something of a religious nature from our culture. He went back to the workshop to store my holy book next to his other items of faith. They both expressed how grateful they were for the gift.

Malik got word of my departure and didn't like the surprise. He was hoping for a more formal send off with gifts and food. He came back to our office trailer with a small desktop notepad holder he wanted me to have as a gift. He explained to me it was a memento he had gotten when he went to Egypt years ago. The brown, leather cover had a gold-stamped profile of an Egyptian Pharaoh on the cover and looked handmade. I could tell it was a treasured personal possession of his and really didn't want to accept it from him. But it was all he had, and I wanted to be a gracious guest. So, I gave the standard answer of "This isn't necessary," while I accepted the item with thanks. The exchange was so humbling I teared up and turned my head. Where else in this world would people of such simple means share their precious possessions with those they have known for only a few months?

It didn't take long before everyone stopped work and a crowd began to gather. Most everyone that I was used to seeing throughout the workdays came to wish me off. Despite the ever-present language barrier, they somehow communicated to me that they hoped that all of us contractors and our security teams would return. They expressed how thankful they were to all of us for leaving the safety of our homes and helping them rebuild this power plant equipment. We all convened at the office trailer to get some group pictures About twenty-six Iraqis showed up, along with me and Brent.

For me, the few pictures we took are a moment in time that I can never forget. Although I was excited to go home, there was an overwhelming feeling when all these men of such a different culture had gathered on my behalf to bid farewell. It was very difficult to say goodbye. I used the rationale that I would be back to soften the blow to my Iraqi friends and to myself. After handshakes and embraces, we exchanged some phone numbers and addresses, then we left the plant, heading back to camp at the base.

I didn't say a word all the way back. One would think I would have been as chipper as a lottery winner. But the overall human experience in Iraq was so rich for me that leaving these friends caused an inner turmoil that I hadn't expected. So, I leaned heavily on the fact that I would return in February. I had just completed spending a total of 105 days in Iraq working side by side with the average working-class Iraqi people. On the way back, we saw a horde of kids playing a soccer game in a makeshift dirt field. This was a first. Never had we seen children playing en masse like this. And the immediate thought that ran through my mind was, "*Ta-del-el*," as I had learned earlier from Malik which means, "It will be all right."

CHAPTER 9

The return trip to Kuwait was uneventful. The day was cold and cloudy with intermittent periods of strong, windswept rain. I was the only contractor returning to Kuwait that day, but the border trip for me would still be by armored vehicle team instead of military flight. There hadn't been a mortar or rocket attack since mid-October, and roadside bombs against convoys had dropped to zero for several weeks along Tampa down to the Kuwait border. The small children at the border parking area showed up, and I felt bad that I forgot to pick up some goodies for them. I rummaged through the trucks and managed to scrounge up a couple cans of soda and some chewing gum for them. My transfer from an armed security team to the Kuwait City–bound unarmed security team went down without any issues, and we even were waved through Kuwait customs. That meant I didn't have to dump out all my gear while they looked for the typical contraband that people often tried to sneak in, specifically booze and sexually explicit magazines. Kind of embarrassing though. Here we were, helping to rebuild an oppressed society, yet we were known to import portions of our culture that they perceived as pernicious to their own. Both Iraqis and Kuwaitis shun alcohol and sexual promiscuity, although alcohol is legally available in Iraq. We went through the final gate checks of an American checkpoint with a quick vehicle inspection, and that was the extent of it. I was back in the world of breathing easy.

It's difficult to describe the experience of living in a hostile environment. Every minute you are there is time spent close to Heavenly Father with thoughts about the plan of salvation and the grand scheme of things predominating within one's mind. There is a higher probability that life can be taken at any moment, so an awareness of the fragile nature of mortality becomes the catalyst for constant spiritual reflection. Just as the scriptures demonstrate, with tribulation, we become closer to God; with peace and prosperity, we tend to drift away. And as we've learned from Nephite history, this applies to nations as well as individuals.

Adjusting to life outside of Iraq took time, and I started off immediately as I spent the next two days in an upscale Kuwait hotel before flying back to the US. Abundant gourmet food was always available, as were rich, calorie-laden desserts. For middle-aged men that fight weight gain, that can mean the risk of recreational eating is high. It was a sharp contrast to the camp life in which all of us contractors and security personnel ate reasonable meals and drank plenty of water. As I sat in this breathtaking Kuwait hotel dining area, a backroom kitchen door would pound out a low frequency thump while servers went in and out. Each thump was reminiscent of a mortar or rocket strike, and I could not adjust. The reaction at each impact was a surge of adrenaline and a sweat flash that occurred immediately.

Regardless of the serenity of the environment, I couldn't control this reaction. It was involuntary.

I found myself being more patient, aware, and cautious. While shopping at a Kuwaiti store, I wasn't at all embarrassed to stare back at local men who looked me over. In the past, I would just make brief eye contact, then dismiss the attention. Now I had enlarged my mistrusting nature to the point where I didn't want a taxi ride and I even looked over my shoulder a couple times during the brief walks from the hotel. But my patience had grown, and my compassion for those at the lower tiers of society was changing.

On departure day at Kuwait International Airport, I had an interesting experience with some UK passengers while checking in baggage at the ticket counter. As people were dropped off at the departure gates, a bag handler would swiftly approach and begin to load your luggage onto roll carts and escort you to security and the ticket counter. All the men were expatriates, usually smaller than a typical American male, and seemed to be mostly of Bangladeshi descent, or so I was told. In a rush and not knowing if this was an airport provided service or not, I obliged him and went through security screening with his assistance. After his service was complete, he used broken English to ask for several hundred fils of Kuwaiti money. Because I didn't have any Kuwaiti currency and I felt a little swindled, I brushed him off using the money as an excuse. I never really asked him for his service, and I was distracted by time constraints. He left without incident. But two UK men came up behind me several minutes later and thought it was worth a disturbance to avoid paying for the unsolicited service. They made such a scene and were so proud of themselves that it bothered me, and now I felt bad. My opportunity to administer of my substance unto one that stands in need was missed. Once I realized it was only about two US dollars they were asking for, I felt even worse. One of the UK men looked right at me as if for a nod of approval, and I said, "For two bucks, why not just give him the money and be done with it?" He blasted me, saying, "Typical American response to buy your way out of every situation." So, I just kept my mouth shut. *Why even try?* I thought.

As soon as check-in was complete, I found the porter who had helped me and gave him several US dollars. I hoped he would forgive me and understand how to exchange it for Kuwaiti currency. He looked a little confused but took the bills regardless. "Give to every man that asketh of thee," the scriptures tell us, yet I was too busy to oblige this man. In this case, I did receive a service and should have been impressed that these men did indeed work for their wages. But why the callous attitude from the others? What causes this reaction, and why did I begin this journey being selfish myself? Was I just too busy to stop my agenda and have compassion? Why let pride and money tarnish one's conduct? I decided to slow down and look at each human crossroad as a divine test just as I had done with my Iraqi friends. The scripture in Hebrews 13 came to mind again. *It applies everywhere, not just in Iraq,* I thought. I was not back in my world very long and already I had blinders on to those around me. Perhaps prosperity does cause compassion to become brittle. My motto for dealing with tips for service and such is now summed up by the simple phrase, "I have it, and they need it." And I always give whatever is proper.

The flight home continued the adjustment process for me. I was firmly back in a different world now, but it was my world. I was familiar with it but somehow detached. The layover at London Heathrow Airport allowed me to shop a little and to relax and watch people. Watching an Orthodox Jewish family contend with their small flock of children in the busy terminal reminded me that families are the basic unit of all the world's societies. The mom had her hands full, nothing much different than any other family in the world. I wondered when the gospel would be accepted by these descendants of Abraham as well as my Iraqi friends. As I saw other nationalities, I thought about the ten thousand high priests from each tribe of the house of Israel and how they are still yet to organize. Sitting next to an older British woman in the terminal, we struck up conversation about her family and how excited she was to go off to visit them this holiday season. I listened and smiled as I thought about Christmas season and a grand reunion with my family. It occurred to me how especially important family is to the elderly of all cultures.

Upon reaching home and going through customs, I worried about getting my dried dates through. It was so important to me to have those dates. Not because they were good but because they were a gift from a friend in Iraq, and it was tangible evidence of the Iraqis' giving and gracious nature. The dates made it through. The Department of Agriculture attendant joked that I must have had the "Garden Tour," and she didn't even make me dig them out of my carry-on luggage.

At the international arrivals section, I was met by my smiling children waving a banner and a teary-eyed wife who had gallantly ran the household since my departure. It was so strange to be back and just pick up where I had left off over a hundred days earlier. Getting in the van and driving home, just like that. It was too simple. As we drove home, the kids started conversations and excitedly interrupted each other. Then they started to bicker. It was real, and I was home. My wife perceptively said I would be needing to adjust to home life again.

But my personal attitude was changed. I looked at things differently. Many things now seemed petty to me. Vanity became obvious. Worries about fashions and comfort almost annoyed me. Inconveniences didn't really frustrate me as they had in the past. Being with an oppressed people who had so little and yet were still grateful had given me a relative base for comparison of our standards of living. And I became keenly aware of the levels of satisfaction around me—or should I say dissatisfaction? After my time in Iraq, I found I could no longer disassociate dissatisfaction from ingratitude. The comparison I now had wasn't just the standard of physical living, it was a difference in attitude and appreciation. We live in a nation of the "haves," but for a brief time, I'd experienced a degree of the "have nots." What was heart-rending to me was that my Iraqi friends should be living as a society of the "haves," or at least close to it. Especially considering the critical service they perform in their domestic electricity industry. So, I was now referencing everything back to my Iraqi friends, lifestyle, and attitude. It wasn't possible to just turn off the Iraqi experience and pick up where I left off. Just as with my "mortar-thumping" reaction in Kuwait, it was involuntary.

Plenty of ward members were glad to see me back in one piece my first Sunday at church. It was deeply humbling to take the sacrament after having had no contact with Latter-day Saints since leaving the US in September. There was no great fanfare and talks to give or firesides to speak at. Others in the ward and stake had been on military assignments in Iraq and were returning safely. When ward members asked any questions about my experience, I had a difficult time elaborating. It took time to relate the experiences I had just been through to my wife and family, let alone neighbors and church members. I slowly confessed to my wife about the two road bomb events and described the sincere concern we were shown by the workers. She was impressed by the compassion of Malik and the others and was quite relaxed about the incidents.

But I still struggled with any descriptions about my experience. How does one describe the balance of life hanging on the edge pending a mortar strike, rocket attack, or roadside bomb? How could I explain what it feels like to have Iraqi men saying prayers for you, Mohammad and the guys asking if they could guard us somehow, the goose bumps when Malik and I discussed the significance of Abraham, or Galib shedding tears at my departure? Describing feelings can be significantly more difficult than describing events. What caused my encounter with the locals to be different? And was it different? Were the other contractors experiencing similar acceptance? I just didn't know. So, I settled on a standard-type soundbite, saying how grateful the Iraqis are for our help and that I might be going back.

I returned home only a few days before Christmas Eve. About mid-morning on Christmas Day our second phone line rang with the caller ID indicating "Unknown Caller." Picking it up, I was expecting a computer-generated solicitation call of some type and was wondering why these things were being done on Christmas. Instead, a scratchy, muffled voice on the phone proclaimed, "Merry Christmas, how are you and your family?" It was Malik and all the guys in the workshop! They had stayed late at the shop, gathered around, and figured out how to call my house using one of their newly acquired cell phones. I was ecstatic! They all banded together to wish me and my family a merry Christmas. I could hear many of the guys in the background speaking their broken English Christmas greetings, and several "Salaam Alikume, Mr. Mark" phrases were hurled over toward the phone. My wife couldn't believe it! Our kids slowly started to migrate into the room after they heard me speaking loudly. In quiet amazement, they watched me conclude my conversations with many thanks and a few Arabic phrases I had learned. The kids couldn't believe that people from Iraq were calling our house, wishing us a merry Christmas, and asking how we were doing.

For so long I had been working as an engineer on machinery and equipment. But now it dawned on my family how much I work with people too. There was a new human connection made. Now my children knew that these people from Iraq had names, they had families with children, and they seemed to be happy people. Even my wife commented that she could tell they were good men by looking at their eyes. I had scores of pictures we had been looking through since I got home and that was her first comment. So, my Iraq experience had now penetrated my family over and above my stories, pictures, and recollections. It was an awakening to my children and a true cultural benefit that this simple phone call from Malik and the guys accomplished. And the word spread out quickly because teenagers talk. When some of the ward teenagers would come by our house and offer greetings to me, they'd quiz me to verify the fact that my Iraqi friends had called our house. I guess they weren't really sure if my kids were telling the straight story.

But a pleasant surprise came to us when our soon-to-be-twelve-years-old daughter participated in our ward New Beginnings ceremony. All the girls went up one by one to be spotlighted and then share a short, personal story of a significant event in their life. Most of the girls described a cute or humorous circumstance they found themselves in at one time or another. When our daughter got up, her personal story was that she was grateful that her dad could go to Iraq to help the people, that he got home okay, that they were nice people, and that "they even call our house." I was a little shy at the recognition but proud of my daughter. She could have gone on about her dad did this and her dad did that—all the glory to her dad. Or she could have related one of the many cute events in her life. But she was affected by the current events of our family. She had been listening to my feelings about the people there and how I was treated by them. And she was able to discern for herself the goodness of my Iraqi friends and wasn't embarrassed to proclaim it in public.

Time kept its constant beat, and before long, the holidays concluded, and the children were back in school. We attended a ward social for adults with karaoke and dancing. Once again, my mind couldn't disengage from my Iraqi friends throughout the whole social. All I could think of was how I would love to have just one family from Iraq in attendance to demonstrate to them how much clean fun we have as church members. For us as Westerners, it is sad to say but sobriety and faith in God is over-shadowed by our culture of carnal-minded media and indulgent excesses that have stereotyped us. Many times, I would try to explain to my Iraqi hosts that a particular behavior in regard to alcohol, language, fidelity, and the sanctity of our body was not good, and actions were accountable to God. It was probably difficult for them to imagine a worldwide church based in America that believed in these principles and practiced them. Maybe they thought it was just me, and I was an unusual case. Malik and I had that good discussion one day during the month of Ramadan as I scrolled through the Church website for him. But I didn't know if any of those details were getting back to all the guys. Or if Malik could even recall many details about the Church because there was so much information I gave him.

So, I began to torment myself that I hadn't done enough missionary work. It would have been easy for me to give out a case of Arabic copies of the Book of Mormon the day I left or even after I had been there for a few weeks. I still didn't know if there were any guidelines for missionary work in Iraq. There are Christians in the country, but perhaps it's cultural protocol not to proselyte to Muslims. That day when everyone crowded around reading my holy book, I got nervous because of the commotion. Maybe the Holy Ghost was telling me something. Milk before meat perhaps? Or is it that the Lord's house is a house of order and to just hand out many copies of the Book of Mormon to an infant nation wasn't proper protocol? I really didn't know. It was too late now, regardless, but I was trying to develop a plan for this for when I returned in the spring. But just how grandiose should one get?

Then a piece of the spiritual puzzle was delivered to me. One of our stake high council speakers was giving the talk during Sacrament service. As usual, he was not getting my full attention. I perked up when he talked about the witness of Christ and that the Holy Ghost is the witness of Christ. I realized that it is our example and our countenance that performs missionary work also. I settled up with myself that I had done my best, and that courtesy, compassion, and friendship are important missionary tools. Even if it's as simple as a smile and a wave.

I stayed off the work rolls for several weeks, hiding out at home while waiting for specifics on my return trip to Iraq. My wife and I watched the news reports out of Iraq every day. Of course, the drama of the elections predominated, and we speculated what the results would be. January 30 came, and we watched carefully to see the turnout. I was hoping to get a fair version from the major media outlets.

Then I got a communication I didn't expect. A text message came through my cell phone while I was anxiously waiting for news reports. It was Jwad from his cell phone. He typed, "Hello Mark ha be-be (friend), How are familee? I 'choose the best by election. I need see you, all miss you." I was relieved to get word all were safe, and at least I knew some of them had participated in the elections on Sunday. After learning of the successful turn-out in the Iraq election, we eagerly awaited for President Bush to give the State of the Union address on Wednesday. My wife and I watched intently while the president spoke. When Safia Taleb al-Suhail, leader of the Iraqi Women's Political Council, stood up and showed her purple, ink-stained finger to the pres-ident (proving she had voted), the emotions overwhelmed the both of us. The high turnout and knowing that several times I sat in that workshop and encouraged these brave men to vote made the risk worth it.

After the elections, I communicated more frequently with my Irish and Scottish colleagues concerning returning to Iraq to complete our projects. Phone calls and emails back and forth from across the Atlantic became a daily occurrence. But some-thing different was going on with the corporate side this time. Because of corporate divisions of responsibility, it was beginning to appear that I would be requested to work at the plant my Scottish colleague worked at before and he would be working at my plant. We both thought this decision was foolish. Both of us knew exactly where we left off before Christmas regarding the plant each of us had worked at.

There was another significant change this time too. The US government entity with overall project responsibility had declined to allow the existing contract to continue with additional funding. A new contract was in place between the US government and their preferred contractor. It would specify them as the prime contractor for this job, and we would be subcontracted by them. I alerted Malik and the others through text messages that I was being asked to go to the other plant. Soon I arranged a phone call to Galib. My brother-in-law is of Lebanese descent and speaks Arabic and has several friends in my area who could help interpret for me. We set up a late evening time, and I went to this friend's house. I knew Galib's exact movements around the plant, and we dialed up so he would answer when he was right near the workshop. We connected, and Galib passed the phone around for several minutes. I had a whirlwind of excited greetings with most of the guys. After some back and forth describing the issue using my Arabic translator, the guys said just to come. We would work on switching after I got there. It was funny: I finally had a dedicated translator at my disposal, and the guys still were anxious to talk to me at every chance throughout the conversation. I had to tell my translator friend a couple times to wait as he would say to me, "Here, they want to talk to you again."

The phone call cut out early, but our major communications were a success. My translator and his wife were softened by the exchange too. I knew that there was some previous exasperation from this married couple about the US presence in the Arab world. But after talking with Galib and listening to the others in the background, these folks changed their thinking process and started to show a little more approval of the Iraqi invasion. It's remarkable how an opinion can be changed or a perception shattered when the human-to-human experience intervenes.

I was somewhat uneasy about the way the whole corporate episode was unfolding, but I wanted to come back to finish the project and work with the guys again. Malik had made contact with the new prime contractor and requested that I come back to his facility to complete the project. He wasn't getting much response, and I later found out it was my company management that wasn't interested in responding to Malik's request. But something else was changing this time. Our corporate management wanted me to interface directly with them and oversee the project. I would be responsible to the prime contractor and to them. Specific definitions of responsibilities were vague at this point, but my primary motivation was still to return and be reunited with my friends. So, I agreed to go regardless of the changes and started to make preparations to return.

My first order of business was to bring gifts back for all the men, their wives, and their children. This ended up being an extremely rewarding task that our whole family took on. For the next couple of weeks, every trip to Wal-Mart, Target, or even Home Depot had everyone looking at things and suggesting, "Dad, you need to bring one of these back to them," or "Dad, do you think they have these over there?" We were trying to decide what they had access to and what they didn't. It was a great family experience. And it was the opposite of a Christmas shopping venture where young minds get quickly distracted and concern themselves with only what they want for gifts. Our children were learning about giving and how to truly put away selfish desires to focus on others. At least that's what my wife and I would like to think. Since Christmas had just passed, maybe the kids already had their fill of gifts for the time being.

The gift selection process finally ended. I printed out a quality copy of the Imam Ali portrait from the digital image Jwad and Ayad had me download in Iraq and had some help from our kids putting them into small, wooden frames. The guys were set with a nice hand tool bag with the small-framed portrait of Imam Ali. For the wives, we thought some fragrant hand cream would be nice, along with many types of small stuffed animals and small racecars for the children. I remembered the dry-erase boards and decided to get one each for Mohammad and Omar, the two engineers, as well as one for Malik. And I bought a large package of Nicorette gum, debating with myself who needed it the most.

An amusing incident with the hand creams took place. After my wife laboriously selected different fragrances from a Victoria Secret shop and brought them home, I started to read the titles on each tube. As per the trendy styles of these days, there were a few of them that sounded just too carnal for Islamic culture. Names such as "Pure Seduction" and "Forbidden Fantasy" just didn't seem right. The head of the house and I debated on this. If they got the English interpretation of these names, I would be embarrassed. It made sense. So, I won out on this one, was installed back as head of the house, and was promptly sent off to the mall for replacements with more safe and neutral titles such as "Pear Glaze" and "Endless Love."

We worked together and the kids helped a little with the sorting and packing of each tool bag. I carefully packed them in my "gift luggage" while starting to stress out about my own gear. My oldest son and I disassembled one of our older computers, and we removed the video card and memory chips because I knew Jwad had a computer, and he could use the components to upgrade his system.

Time never paused, and departure day was coming soon. I sheepishly let ward members know I was going back to Iraq, and my wife invited people over for a combination birthday and send-off gathering for me. As we gathered that evening in little pockets of discussion, I described how I really felt about the people there, my personal role in what was happening, and the ease with which our family felt about my return. My conversations that evening weren't in defense of being crazy for returning, they were about the human interactions I was able to experience. It was difficult to explain the personal reward and that it might not be available any other time in my life. There was a complete ease about returning, except for the uncertainty about whether I would be working with my previous friends at their plant.

This time around, as the departure day drew closer, I felt prepared. There were the gifts to give, plenty of items for my personal comfort were packed, and I knew where I was going and hopefully what to expect. The same comfortable flight to London then Kuwait was scheduled. It was all routine now. Then, some last-minute revelations were passed down to me from management in the Middle East offices. The security team relationships had been altered. Our crackerjack security team would be reduced to an advisor status. The prime contractor would be supplying the main security contractor and transportation, and our advisor would accompany each group of contractors to the plant and remain with us throughout the day. This amounted to a security advisor for our interests along with the prime contractor's team. While I didn't know how this would work out on a practical basis, it sounded reasonable. I was set to go, and changes in conditions were inconsequential to me at this point. If our corporate security deemed the remobilization was unsafe, then the trip would be aborted, and I would trust them to make that decision. This new security structure was good information to have to avoid surprises, and I appreciated the communications.

Airport goodbyes were not as apprehensive as on my first trip. To the contrary, there was complete ease and excitement with my wife and children this time. Because my family had been involved beforehand, they'd come to view this trip as a way to help people. The first trip they just viewed as Dad going to Iraq. Again, it is noteworthy how attitudes change when the human connection is established. Faces now accompanied names and even a few voices. So, with cheerful attitudes and a personal stake in the success, my family put me on the plane with tears, waves, and kisses blown from cupped hands. Most ward members knew nothing special except that I was returning to finish the original project. For me, I was returning to see friends, help people, and work hard. At least that's what I thought as I got on the airplane.

CHAPTER 10

With many of the unknowns eliminated, getting back to Kuwait and its plush accommodations seemed effortless this time. Communications were prompt upon arrival and entrance into Iraq was scheduled for within the next forty-eight hours. An armored vehicle team from our advisor security contractor would be responsible for our transport all the way to the contractor camp at the Coalition base. The entire team of three Americans, including myself, and three Filipinos would make the crossing. A Scottish man would be arriving later within two weeks. The Filipino workers had been held back in Kuwait for almost two weeks pending arrival of the entire team. By this point, they were going a little stir crazy, and they were glad to see things finally get underway. One of these men was a worker who'd been dismissed the previous fall. He was also like me in that he wanted to go back to the same site as last fall but had been assigned differently. Neither of us had a clue why this was. We both had a strong desire to work with the guys again at the old plant. We both agreed it should all work out for the best and just getting there again would be a major accomplishment.

The border run was set, and our familiar security contractors efficiently communicated to us the timing, plans, and expectations dealing with our crossing. The weather was going through its seasonal change, and everyone was back in short-sleeved shirts and jeans. Those cold days of December had left a strong impression in my mind, but now it was the last few days of February, and the harsh desert landscape was different this time. The bulk of Kuwait was green. The fruit trees, landscaping, and grass was lush and colorful. Ornate flowering bushes and other landscaping plants adorned the shops, hotels, and office buildings in and around Kuwait City. As we began our trip north to the border crossing near the town of Safwan, I saw a similar transformation of the Kuwaiti desert. Many flocks of sheep were grazing. A large herd of camels were being escorted by young ranch hands on foot with older men wearing traditional Arab garb and driving well-kept, four-wheel-drive Toyota and Nissan pick-up trucks. On my earlier trips through this desert, all I'd seen was the cruel, scorching brutality of nature in September and then the dreary, damp cold of December. This trip I saw more life and human involvement. The desert land did express some character, after all.

At the physical border there was another difference. The huge parking lot of convoy trucks was full to capacity, and the border procedures were more structured. In addition, there was a newly designated route through an American checkpoint before entrance into Iraq. Our security men had a more stringent check-in procedure to follow, and we waited longer at the entrance station while they validated our credentials. Entrance was granted, and we traveled the short distance to the transfer point, switching into armored vehicles after we donned our body armor.

The three little girls and little boy ran up to the vehicles as we pulled in. Once again, I'd forgotten to bring treats, but so did everyone else in the team. We managed to come up with an impressive mix of sodas, fruit, and a couple of candies between us. There was much more activity in the area this time. Many more groups of security teams were in small enclaves with their armored vehicles. There seemed to be more Iraqi men toting weapons and wearing body armor, all under hire from the numerous private security firms. It didn't seem quite as primitive this time. There was more organization to deal with the increased activity. The area even looked as though someone had picked up some of the trash and debris.

Our drive to the Coalition base used the same route on Tampa as before. The massive road collapse from the pipeline sabotage near Basra was still in a state of disrepair. But the detour was more well-defined, and usage had increased. There was an orderly line of local and military traffic slowly moving through the now-smoothed-out detour. Construction crews had cleaned out the bombed-out sections of asphalt and were making preparations toward permanent repair. As we continued northward, I noticed all the small farms were thriving with green rows of open vegetation. Later, I learned it was predominately tomato plants in the far south and that the area was recognized for its abundant spring crops. Other sites were familiar yet displayed a seasonal change as we drove up toward the base. The landscape didn't appear quite as harsh and foreboding as the last trip.

Arriving at the contractor camp, I found almost everything in the same state as when I left in December. My new room was right next to the old one from the first trip. Many of the same faces were in the camp, cleaning the rooms, doing the laundry, and cooking the food. We had a small reunion at camp, and most of us were back in the mindset of working hard and completing the tasks.

A quick meeting was called with our new prime contractor leader and his security leader for our projects. There had been a recent security event at our particular plant, which would delay our return. A local security contractor had been inspecting the outside perimeter at the plant when he came under small arms fire. All the contractor teams were extracted immediately and returned to the Coalition base until further notice. We'd been at the contractor camp for just a few hours when this event took place. Security declared a lockdown status and confined us to the base until proper measures were taken to reduce or eliminate the threat.

At this point, the first defensive measure was going to be a complete series of cement blast-wall sections constructed around the perimeter of the entire plant. Construction of this wall might take as long as three weeks and would restrict us from the plant until completion. I asked about the possibility of going to the other site to see my friends. There wasn't much give with any of these new managers but rightly so. Why take any extra risks? People were getting shot at, and there were security resource issues from this new security contractor already. As I already knew from the previous experiences, the terrain was so rough on the heavy-armored vehicles that vehicle failures were high. It wasn't feasible to just tag along for a day or so.

My Scottish, Irish, and Pakistani colleagues were already making appearances at Malik's plant and beginning a tough schedule to completion. The messages back from these men every evening was that the Iraqi guys would ask every day when I would be coming to their plant for work. I kind of felt like a high school student whose best friend was dating an ex-girlfriend that jilted me and I had to hear about her every day. I asked the prime contractor if I could work at the other site but was met with resistance, and my own company had no intention of going along with changes either. It was a given that I'd be working at the other plant. But there were some positives. The distance from camp to the other plant was closer, there was added security, and I would be meeting new people. I also tried to look for a spiritual insight and finally ended up with the same outlook my Iraqi friends had taught me last year: the Arabic phrase "*Inshallah*," which means "God willing." One just submits to circumstances because it's God's will. *And who are we to know otherwise*, I thought.

Any contribution to our project work effort while confined in camp wasn't significant. On the contrary, the three of us Americans tried to fill in the time by exercising and taking small trips within the base to break up the monotony of the camp. One on-base excursion found us exploring deep inside one of the old Iraqi bomb bunkers not damaged during any of the hostilities. It was a maze of Russian-made hatchways and bulkheads presumably from the Soviet ship industry. There was plenty of evidence that Coalition forces had been in there recently, including atropine and other US and UK chemical agent protective devices discarded in the corners. Elaborate ventilation systems with rudimentary Russian-made motors and fans had provided all the technology to keep things flowing in the past. Now it was just broken equipment that looked as if it has been dormant for many years.

On another trip we ventured deep inside some kind of jail or very tall confinement building. It was a crudely erected brick-and-mortar structure with a tin, sheet-metal roof and dirt floor. There appeared to be a solitary confinement section with only one passageway at ground level about two-by-two foot with a locking metal hatchway on hinges. The total floor space seemed about a ten-foot-by-ten-foot floor square on the inside. The entire building gave us an uneasy feeling, so we only spent a short amount of time in there.

Regardless of the free time, the personal frustration got to the point where I just wanted to see the guys one more time, give them the gifts, and then just leave Iraq entirely. Day after day of camp confinement was starting to get on our nerves. The Filipino workers were also getting antsy. We were all starting to go nuts.

But finally, a plan was made to allow me go Malik's plant for a day. I anxiously organized all the gifts in the gift luggage the night before and was taken out the next day. This was my first trip outside of the base, and it was noticeably different this time. We were accompanied by Iraqi National Guard troops with new automatic weapons and dressed in clean, desert-colored fatigues. No scary-looking black ski masks this time. They drove new, desert-camouflaged, small troop carriers with Arabic letters on the sides and the English letters "ING." This time around, there was no more potentially infuriating road blocking. These men would stop and jump out at intersections and direct traffic for us. It was all done in an orderly fashion. We arrived safely and in good time. When we arrived, we had a great reunion as everybody gathered together. I wasn't at all embarrassed to make such a scene. After greetings were complete, I had some work items to look at and we agreed to meet for lunch in the workshop.

It was good timing because the guys were just concluding their prayers as I came in for lunch. Although I had been present so many times before during their prayers, I noticed that each man had a small disk and would bow his head all the way to the ground, touching his forehead on the disk. Jwad saw that I was interested and showed me his disk, then offered it to me as a gift. Shiite prayers use this small disk, which is made from mud taken from nearby Karbala and is imprinted with a drawing of a mosque on one side. It is considered a holy token from the battle scene where historical Shiite figures were slain and laid to rest. I was grateful for this small token and surprised I hadn't noticed it before. In the past, I think I was trying to be reverent and would always step out or try to avoid staring at them during their prayers. But being in their presence this time while they said their prayers brought back that unique feeling of God-fearing men humbly unashamed of their belief in deity.

Lunch was prepped and spread out, and we all sat down and ate together. It was good times again, and we joked and laughed with Galib, Mohammad, and Malik there to clarify the English. They told me they'd all voted in the elections and were proud to have done so. Basically, they followed the advice of their cleric Ali Sistani except for Galib who voted for the communist-affiliated candidate. Malik didn't comment, and I thought he'd probably chosen different than the mainstream. There were some insurgent incidents in the region on election day that they knew of, but none at their particular polling place.

We caught up, and I handed out my gifts one by one as we finished up the eating. As I gave out the nicotine gum to the smokers and told them to share, they had to figure out what it was. There was some anxious discussion among them at first, then a little scolding from their non-smoking workmates for smoking in the first place. Everyone agreed the Nicorette gum was a useful and clever gift. The items for the wives and children were a pleasant surprise to them. I came up short on hand creams for Tariq "Two Wives," and he just handed back the single tube to me. When I asked him if only one hand cream was "*mush-killa*" (problem), he raised an eyebrow and mimicked cutting the tube in half with his fingers. "Yes, big problem," he said, and we immediately roared in laughter. I felt bad since he was so generous with the kilo of dates he had given me to take home at Christmas. We agreed to wait until my wife could send a few more tubes to me, and he would distribute them evenly.

Everyone was grateful beyond measure and didn't expect anything. Malik told me that I didn't have to do this for the children and all. My response to him was that I only wished they could have the prosperity, the freedoms, and the joy that I had. They confessed they had gotten something for me and that they had been anxiously saving it for several weeks now. It was large and wrapped in brown paper. I didn't know what to expect and was perturbed because they had spent hard-earned money on me with their phone calls already. Galib made a trip over to Babylon weeks before to pick up a brass embossing of the winged lion of Babylon for me. It was in a framed setting about fifteen-by-eighteen inches with about a two-inch thickness. It was gorgeous and unique, and today is one of my most precious reminders of my time in Iraq. I had to look away to avoid my eyes tearing up while I unwrapped this gift in the absolute stone silence of all the guys watching. They rolled off into conversation among themselves after they could see my sincere appreciation. I could tell they were all excited that they had chosen a very meaningful gift for me.

All of us were sad to see the conclusion of this day. Actually, my visit had caused a break from routine, and the day was a semi-wash as far as getting significant work accomplished. Toward the end of this social event, some of the guys raised concern about the lack of cordial communication from some of these new prime contractors on site. One of the new managers walked through the workshop while we were in the midst of socializing and looking over our gifts. He kind of looked in then walked through and left. Immediately after this man left, Ayad asked me, "Mr. Mark, why no salaam Alikume?" A couple of the other guys piped in and said, "Mush-killa?" I just wasn't sure what to say, so I told them, "Maybe not happy." Ayad went on saying, "Everyday no salaam Alikume," then Ayad frowned to indicate a problem. But the feeling of the guys was not fear, anger, or intolerance of any kind. They worried it was something they had done and were discussing ways to make this man comfortable while he was in Iraq. They were concerned if they could make him content somehow. I was always amazed at how these Iraqi men would notice these things and be so perceptive. My initial reaction to any social introvert is that there could be hidden problems and perhaps it's best to stand back for now. But once again, my Iraqi hosts demonstrated their tolerant and forgiving nature. Unlike me, my Iraqi friends didn't want to remove this gentleman from the job or stand back cautiously. They were concerned if they could help change his mood for the better.

Several of these new contractors weren't quite as solemn as that one man, so there was a balance. Although it's possible I was the only Western contractor to frequently sit down and eat and engage in discussion with them, I learned that the guys were just as cordial and inviting to the others as they were to me. More than once, it occurred to me that maybe contractors should go through some degree of screening to ensure they have some basic social skills, especially when working in any culturally sensitive area. However, people have their problems, and this is part of life's challenges. Dealing with our own issues as well as helping those around us is part of the eternal plan. How we conduct ourselves is part of the test. How we react to others is another test too. I can honestly say that my Iraqi friends passed that test without issue.

The day was over, and we agreed there would be some visits from them while I was working at the other plant. Upon return to camp that evening, the news was out that our security wall was nearing completion, and we would commence work shortly. It had been quiet for weeks now without any insurgent activity and confidence was high. All of us that had been camp bound were anxious to start a routine. My communications with the corporate folks had been no more than a scratchy phone call a day to check the status. And there weren't enough activities taking place to develop any type of relationship or to get a sense of their competence as management. What I did know about them was the usual. A young professional was designated as site manager and working the office side from a Middle East office in a UAE location. He would be my interface point, and I had been given a cell phone to communicate with him upon arrival at camp weeks earlier. The more experienced management presided as a project management team in the form of a committee from US offices. One individual was designated as the overall project manager. A significant change this time was the relationship between the prime contractor and us. We were subcontracted to the prime contractor. But I soon learned that my management had difficulty adjusting to this change and conducted themselves as if there were no change from the previous and now expired contract.

Our plant was finally granted security clearance, and the short ride to the facility from the base was uneventful. The initial trip for us was somewhat round about. Our new security contractor wasn't too familiar with the area and struggled with the short drive from the Coalition base to the plant. There was a large refinery of some type very near, and as we drove by, I could see the same general, decrepit condition as the other areas of the country. Mounds of junk metal and racks of large, unused, rusted pipe stored haphazardly as if all were just piles of scrap covered the area. As time went on, I started to quiz many of our security men about other areas of Iraq that they had been to. Did the conditions change anywhere? Was the whole country in a state of general neglect and disrepair? They agreed that all they had seen even in Saddam's home region in the Sunni Triangle was similar. The security men told me there were beautiful areas of Baghdad, most notably Dura and Monsier, but impoverished areas were never far away.

The approach to the plant was well fortified with the new, cement blast wall in place, and an impressive army of private security guards with automatic weapons standing sentry and posted throughout. All these men were Iraqi. I had not been there since the roadside bomb went off between our vehicles the past September, and passing by that spot gave me a chilling recall of that event. How could such a device get planted there so close to the plant anyway?

Aside from being a different plant, everything was typical of the other areas I had worked. Same style of run-down housing with adults working in the fields. Children ran up to the side of the road giving thumbs-up. Piles of trash, twisted steel, and garbage were strewn about. There was no dramatic difference between this plant and the other areas. For us, there was a comfort zone once inside the gates, although the high number of Iraqi guards had some of us a little nervous. This particular issue kept coming up among ourselves. But we were adjusting, and the new physical and human structures eventually felt normal. Because of the good experiences all of us had last fall working with the people, we were all okay with Iraqi guards as long as there was some kind of a balance with UK or other non-Iraqi nationals. This is the Iraqis' country after all, and they would become complete custodians of it in due time. So, why not start now? We assumed all the Iraqi security men were local to the region.

Other security protocols had also changed. In addition to the small army of Iraqi men guarding the perimeter, one team of Iraqi men would be in an unarmored vehicle and be a part of our "Call Sign," which was security lingo that described our group of vehicles. They would accompany us to the plant and back as a lead or lag vehicle. One of the more uncomfortable changes was the requirement for contractors to wear our bulky body armor when traversing between the office and the actual generator building. This bothered several of us because we stood out from a distance. But overall, we were moderately comfortable with the arrangement and the ratio of close protection UK-type guards was still near one to one. We still had the presence of our crackerjack professionals from our corporate security division assigned as advisors.

The condition of the plant was like we expected. The older age of the equipment made the area seem more antiquated. Each of the two turbine generator sets was located in the single generator building. One was running and in a similar condition as we had found at Malik's plant on the first trip: noisy, smoking, dirt and burned grease everywhere, ventilation doors removed, makeshift oil catch trays, and at about one-half capacity power production. The other unit was in a partially assembled state and awaited our attention. The back area behind the generator house was littered with old components as well as scrap metal piles from structural steel remnants not related to the power plant.

The plant itself had more landscaping with irrigation and several native trees around the inner perimeter. It gave the area a tropical effect. Despite its smaller geographical size, this site had many plant workers assigned to its workforce and the numbers were difficult to determine. As was typical, many men had menial jobs, but the plant was somewhat cleaner and greener and, except the junk piles in the back, was somewhat taken care of. Much of the trash was on the outside of the plant walls.

There was a small housing complex directly behind us, and we could see the second story of these sandy-colored, adobe-brick buildings from within the plant boundaries. The complex was not quite as primitive as the satellite-equipped mud dwellings further down the road, but it was still not up to the standard of the lesser areas in Kuwait City. Initial contact with the plant workers was positive, and smiles and waves were being dealt out freely. All the plant workers were friendly as we expected, and the plant manager was cordial and invited me and the other contractor staff to come and discuss any matters in his office. Several women were employed there as administrational workers and would scurry past our work areas, not to be seen again until the end of the workday. The left-over contractor office trailer was modified with cement blast walls around the perimeter. An amusing note was left behind from my Scottish colleague explaining the degree of work that required completion and the frustrations that should be expected.

Our prime contractor leader was an older, more experienced American of European descent from the Deep South. He was a little crusty but had good intentions for relations with the local labor as well as being properly enabled for local procurement and tooling needs. Many times, we would lightly discuss the strategy his company assembled to assist the local plant workforce with adequate pay, proper training, and conformance to the guidelines the US government had set for work relations with the Ministry of Electricity. They had hired several men to assist in local purchases of consumable items such as rags, paper, work gloves, and whatever else would be needed. All these procurement specialists spoke some English. Their task was tough at times because our prime contractor leader would gruffly request industrial items he expected them to dig up for us in the local markets.

For an industrialized country such as Iraq, the difficulty of obtaining common items still surprised me. I made a seemingly simple request for hanging folders that took a day or so. What I received was a stack of the most cumbersome, crudely fabricated hanging folders that were stamped with "Made in Syria" in English and Arabic. They looked like some kind of WWII relics with big globs of dried glue and roughly cut, dull metal runners. All seemed to be hand-assembled out of coarse, orange-brownish hardboard. I meant to bring some back home so people would believe me. I couldn't even figure out how to install the monstrous, plastic, clamp-on tags that were supplied with them. Maybe there was some other pieces that went with them that were forgotten.

Other requests for specific items were equally difficult to obtain, and we debated on whether to fly in new items via Baghdad military flights or to keep searching locally. A few times the procurement specialists brought in used items such as gaskets, rubber seals, and fittings for our acceptance. They dealt gamely with a struggling system of commerce on our behalf, and it became interesting to watch the reactions from some of us with the items they would return with. After many days, I got to know the plant workers better and learned that several of them were Christians and local to the region. The morning I discovered that information, I remember them saying, "Is no problem, all Iraqis love each other. Muslim, Christian, whatever, is no problem." There were several other men in the office at that moment, and everyone was nodding their heads in agreement.

Even with all the logistical issues and supply deficiencies, this whole project seemed to be a better setup than my previous run. It was obvious that this prime contractor took full ownership of the project, was better organized for our support, and had the best interests of Iraqi power production as the agenda. From the security standpoint, we all felt a little more exposed initially. But the history of last year was confined to the early roadside bomb incident of which I had an intimate view and another nearby roadside bomb late in November that caused no damage or injuries. All else seemed in order for work to progress this time with experienced staff, local resources, and a secured worksite. The sniper fire that prompted the perimeter wall construction seemed to be an isolated event and was out of our minds by this time.

For me, it was going to be difficult to duplicate my experience from the first trip. As corporate leader on this venture, I wasn't going to be able to spend time with the workers as I had before. Learning their names and discussing politics, culture, and religion wasn't going to flow naturally this time. However, everyone seemed to know me as I went out into the work areas. But working with the local men shoulder to shoulder was not in my duties this time. So, when our Scotsman arrived, he and the Filipino supervisors were my eyes and ears. The other two Americans were involved exclusively with the electrical portion of the project and worked fairly independently. Since the prime contractor had hired some local talent with good English skills for supervision support, it actually felt like we had a couple of interpreters this time. One of the men I would get to work closely with was Mohammad Ali.

Ali was one of the locals and a capable supervisor, and we ended up conversing together quite often. His English skills, experience, mellow attitude, and mature disposition became invaluable. A gentleman in his mid-fifties, he had all the typical features of the typical Iraqi man from the area, except for being taller than most with a bit more weight on him. He was also totally clean shaven. Many times, he and I would get to drift off from the noisy work area and engage in some personal discussions. I was surprised to find out that he was a divorcé from his first marriage years before. As a civil matter, he was required to pay alimony-type payments as ordered by the Iraqi court. Since there were children involved, the procedures and commitments were very similar to settlements we see in Western society. This was a secular side of Iraqi society that I had not learned much about previously.

And Ali also had plenty of Saddam government stories to share with me. The draining of the wetlands in the south bothered him quite a bit because of the economic hardship it brought to the area. His first wife had been required to participate in a pro-Saddam demonstration one afternoon years ago. Apparently, participation was a rotational-type thing where they called on you at random and you had to attend. Being educated and a bit more exposed to other governments in the region, that incident seemed to aggravate him to a great extent. The intrusion of personal freedoms bothered him severely.

A faithful Shiite that talked fondly about his two teenage girls, he was somewhat a secular-type individual that expressed high hopes of economic prosperity because of the removal of tyranny. He told me that two insurgent rockets had landed nearby while he and his wife were waiting to vote on election day in January 2005. The overall mood of the people at the polling station became a stronger determination to cast their ballots after the rocket attack. He said nobody ran or took cover. Instead, they just reacted with a protective crouch and held their ground, undeterred by the danger.

An optimist, Ali enjoyed a good laugh and told some clean jokes every so often. He always stressed that the bulk of the

Arab world were just good people of the earth. His statements concerning Arab attitude always intrigued me. Given light of the historical changes in Lebanon that were taking place at that very time, I always listened carefully to Ali when he would talk in broad generalizations. He seemed to have a firm grasp on his outlook. We truly enjoyed each other's company. And just like all the men I worked closely with, he desperately wished that I could come to his house for dinner and socializing with his family and friends.

There were many other good, local people in this new structure I got to deal with. The plant manager had other duties in regard to the Ministry of Electricity and was always busy, but he made time for us whenever necessary. The dedicated office trailer cleaning man was always willing to crack a smile and try his English on us. We would offer our extra lunch rations to him, and he would graciously accept with a broad smile and sincere thanks. He would always re-use the black, plastic trash bags that we would supply him for clean-up. We had a tough time breaking him of that habit regardless of how many rolls of new bags we would supply. He was just conditioned to making do with very little. The warehouse attendant was a very religious man and would sing some kind of hymns while I was poking around looking at parts. His small but critical warehouse was always clean and orderly.

One of the plant electrical engineers also spoke English comfortably. We always had good verbal exchanges along with his courteous manner of sharing his excellent knowledge of the plant systems with us. His overall outlook on Iraq and the Arab world was a mirrored reflection of Ali, as were the attitudes of many of the other men that I could communicate with. It was interesting that when conversing with most of these English-speaking men, once business discussions were concluded, the topics would shift to humorous comparisons of family life between us and them or the optimistic future of Iraq. Just as before, everyone craved cultural exchange the most.

There was yet another Iraqi plant electrical engineer who was also a great help and firmly engrossed in the details of the electrical wiring progress of the project. He spoke English well and always welcomed me with a firm handshake while putting his left hand on top of my right in a two-handed-style clasp. Since he was married to two wives, conversations with him always became interesting as talk would drift over to humorous family circumstances. Eventually, he shared some details with me regarding the jealousy of the two separate households of children when they would meet together. Seems that they would get quiet in the presence of each other, then start to complain about the other household when separated. I was honored and privileged as he showed me some photographs of both households. He even had a photo of one wife unveiled, sitting on a very basic, dark. and velvet-looking couch inside a scantly decorated living room. The tile floor seemed to be of a simple construction with a throw rug at the foot of the couch. She had light-colored hair, which surprised me, but I didn't ask any questions about it. Although I'm sure he would have obliged me with an answer, I thought it better to be polite and limit questions. For his family life, apparently keeping the peace was a full-time job. Several of the other plant workers had friends from Malik's plant that would constantly pass on greetings to me from my friends across the desert. So, I would go out to check work progress a few times a day and offer some handshakes and conversation where possible. Shortly into the job, I noticed the Filipinos were only randomly eating lunch in the office trailer with us. Noon hour they could usually be found sitting down in the workshop, enjoying Arabic lunches with the men. Needless to say, I was jealous. My Scottish and American colleagues weren't interested in communal exchanges such as this. To me, it was their loss. All in all, I found the same gracious and friendly attitudes from these Iraqi workers at this new project as I experienced at Malik's plant.

It was getting near time to have a visit from my friends from across the desert. Galib, Mohammad, and Mohammad Two, along with Jwad, were all planning a quick visit any day. When they came, they brought food and some gifts from a couple of the men that weren't there the day I handed out my gifts. A couple of the wives had wrapped up some locally made women's soaps to give to my wife for appreciation of the hand creams. The food they brought was a great treat and included all the foods I had expressed a particular fondness for last year. I thought this was an extremely kind gesture and quite observant of them to remember. Actually, that was quite in their nature to remember my favorites and shower me with calories any chance they could get. I paraded all of them through the work areas to show them our progress. As we went through the very modernized control center, I noticed Jwad eyeing the nice

Dell desktop supplied for data interface. I joked with Jwad and pretended to give him the computer while saying, "Ali-Baba." But Jwad snapped right back saying, "No, Mr. Mark . . . Allah," as he pointed his finger heavenward. Then, we both gave the thumbs-up to each other and nodded our heads in agreement as we walked out of the area.

It was a somewhat rushed visit and the guys started to joke. "Get Mark. Yes, let's kidnap Mark. First, we take him to my house for dinner and meet all my family. Then, your house for sweets and Arabic music. Okay, then back to my house to take pictures and play racecars with children." I caught on to what they were saying and nodded my head. *Yes, I want to go.* We all had a good laugh as I portrayed the American press trying to describe a kidnapped American contractor missing in Iraq but in reality being shuffled from house to house, meeting local families, being stuffed with Iraqi foods, and taking pictures while playing games with their children. It was a conclusion to a great visit and another unforgettable memory of my time in Iraq.

The following couple of weeks we immersed ourselves in the work. A new American named Jim was employed by the prime contractor and came to supervise electrical work. He had been in Iraq earlier for a short period and had limited experience working with the locals, so he was often frustrated by the planning shortfalls dealing with materials and work scheduling. I tried to help Jim see that this wasn't a typical project where we could just FedEx things to the site that we lacked or get new folks from the Union Hall as needed. He began to get vigorous with Mohammad Ali and insert bigger portions on Ali's work plate on a daily basis. It brought Ali and me closer together as I would go out and look for Ali to just visit with him and let him know I was concerned about his stress threshold. Several of the other Iraqi plant engineers were tired as well. It wasn't as much the push as the day after day after day of work. They were exhausted and needed a break. I noticed the prime contractor was more aware of this and began a more culture-considerate policy regarding time off, lunch and prayer break, and some rotational relief for the plant workforce. It all made sense, and I was glad to see this evolution of a gentle coaxing into the demanding routine. Jim eventually felt bad about the demands he had set and backed off. All the Iraqi guys basically endured and kept up with the demands as well as keeping an amiable attitude. It was a typical characteristic of these working-class Iraqi men.

But the Jim experience alerted me to some of the potential shortfalls of quick conversion to American work habits. People become susceptible to mental and physical fatigue and can lose their drive. Sometimes it might be better to explain, educate, and demonstrate to help people adapt to change. I found a very sophisticated ultrasonic parts cleaning apparatus laying in the corner of the plant one day. It had obviously been sent there with the relief goods of repair parts for the power plant equipment. However, this equipment is difficult for me to operate even with proper factory support. So, I thought about the benefit of sending some of the Iraqis to a Western country and letting them see how these items were used. How they were made.

The different applications they could be used for. Let them see how we conducted ourselves at a power plant or a petrochemical complex. Our methods and learning schemes could be valuable training aids for refinement of their own industries. Example is the best teacher. When they could see what we have, they would realize that they could have the same. And the benefit would be for them and their families. Hope is a wonderful principle—it promotes initiative.

As this project progressed, we discovered there was difficulty locating original documentation for some of the critical components and their system descriptions and specifications. We soon discovered that several of the key plant workers were actually guarding many of these technical documents in their homes. The lifestyle they had lived under Saddam was one of uncertainty if the plant would falter. These men took no chances with the security of drawings and systems functional specifications. Eventually, several of the key documents we needed were returned to the plant and allowed us to make progress.

A conversation I had with a couple of the guys told me more about their previous work life than I had known before. Under a threat of the unknown, the guys would perform their jobs to keep the plant running. As I was told before, pay scales under Saddam of three US dollars a month kept incentive low. But fear kept the system from total collapse. Nobody wanted to be in the spotlight for having equipment that didn't operate. To demonstrate the disconnection of the Baghdad regime and reality, the guys told me the story about a high-level government official accompanying one of Saddam's sons into the region several years ago. A steam-energy plant was not operating at maximum and when questioned why this was, the answer was given about the lack of steam. Saddam's son paused for a moment and said something to the effect of "Buy all the steam you can from the local market and get this plant at maximum." But the joke of the story was that nobody in the entourage would correct him. The lack of steam was a technical issue based on equipment ability. So, the consequence of this event was the formalized attitude of every man for himself. It was now easy to understand how critical documents ended up being in private possession. The fear factor was real and existed at the upper levels too.

Despite the prime contractor's sensitive agenda dealing with the locals, our frustration levels with the security teams were starting to increase. The hair-raising but short ride to our plant had a few interesting side trips to keep us awake. In an earlier incident, our sister project got lost on the way back to camp one evening and went through a nearby town that was supposedly off-limits to Coalition forces. As we arrived back at camp that evening, we were treated to the first-hand accounts of this security team and their human cargo of contractors driving through unfamiliar checkpoints. Tales of locals stopping dead in their tracks to stare at the unusual convoy were backed up with some digital photos snapped by one of the American contractors. Trying to envision an entire soccer field filled with players and spectators coming to an abrupt halt as everyone watched the lost security vehicles meander through was easy. The ball kept rolling and was the only thing moving I was told.

Our team also had an unplanned sight-seeing tour into a gated community a few weeks later. We were passed through by the unarmed gate attendant, who even gave us a hello-type wave along with the perplexed look on his face. After figuring out we were bottled in, a quick trip back to the crudely erected gate and exit was granted from our head-scratching gate guard. He even gave us another wave of his hand as we left. In both cases of our security teams straying off the beaten path, none of us saw or felt any immediate threat from the local populace. It just seems to be a form of astonishment, the locals' exhibition of "Wow! Westerners."

But the loosening of security protocols concerned us. There hadn't been a rocket or mortar attack since we had been back in Iraq this time, but it seemed to us that we were starting to get complacent. To add complications to the security environment, four of our local guards from the small army guarding the perimeter turned up missing. No one could account for them. Were they kidnapped, did they quit and go home, or were they murdered? They had critical information on our numbers, schedules, travel routes, and project tasking. This was disturbing to everyone at our site and didn't go over well with our corporate security folks back in the US. We were ordered into lockdown at the Coalition base for a few days while the situation played out. Finally, word came back for us to return to work, and extra precautions would be implemented at our site. All of us agreed and the added measures removed some of the complacency that we felt had developed. Soon we found out that the men were not true local residents and that they had been apprehended by the local Iraqi authorities. They were incarcerated because they weren't locals. The surprise was that the local police weren't being complacent at all. If you were not from around these parts, they hauled you in to check out your story. Seemed that the local police were doing a diligent job at reducing risks, and that the neighborhood watch concept was working.

In the arena of job progress, we were falling behind. Our young site manager located in the UAE began the habit of incessantly calling me on the cell phone. With the lackluster cell connections, these calls became frustrating. He was supposed to be a support mechanism, but I ended up supporting him with a constant feed of written and verbal information. It got to the point where I couldn't support the project with my field skills, and I was getting disconnected from the work. Certain requests from my management regarding scheduling and time accounting relationships with the prime contractor were embarrassing to foster through to the prime contractor leadership for approval. For me, two taskmasters were beginning to emerge. And our less-than-twelve full hours of onsite work time was becoming an issue. Solutions were being drawn to have us working nights to get a full shift on the site. The sad thing about this initiative is that it came from our corporation, the subcontractor. Our own people didn't have confidence in our ability to solve the issues and complete the project within the schedule. They wanted the full twelve hours to be spent onsite. Travel to and from the Coalition base would be during daylight hours.

When informed of this decision the day before, I walked around the plant with our security advisor. He didn't like the arrangement. Portable lighting had been placed throughout the plant effectively illuminating the entire facility interior. We couldn't help but think of the ease with which a rocket or mortar could be aimed our way with the area so well-lit at night. There was corporate debate as to whether we would be allowed to function like this under the prime contractor.

That evening our security advisor and some of his team decided to test the perimeter of the plant by approaching from the outside. Under risk of death, they conducted their probing exercise and successfully made it to the plant walls undetected. The team made a formal plant visit immediately after their little covert mission, then returned to camp. I received informal word from some of our security men that evening not to worry about the nightshift issue. Feedback from our security advisors to their corporate leadership would not favor the facility being deemed safe for night work. The prime contractor security and our security contractor were at odds. So, we stayed in camp the first night under corporate orders and in defiance of our prime contractor while they went to work. It would have been a second night in camp while our prime contractor worked nights, but the word came from our corporate people for us to go to work that evening.

I had vented too much over the phone to my wife in the previous evenings about the whole scenario, and by now, she was worried sick. The adversarial relationship between prime contractor and subcontractor, the continuous barrage of information requests from juvenile management in our corporate chain, and now security concessions. There was even an issue about being paid for travel time en route to the plant and back. Management from my own company in the US explained that travel time from camp to the plant wasn't included as paid hours. Explanations comparing commutes between hotels and worksites were their rationale. I just didn't have the energy to argue, and the prime contractor wasn't behind any of this. Our own corporate people were walking that thin, gray line between greed and self-interest. I realized that the most dangerous time in Iraq is between the gate of the Coalition base and the plant gate, and I was frustrated that the people in corporate didn't want to pay us for it. Regardless of the inconsequential amount of time and money for this travel period, that was the message that this decision sent to us from our own management. It just wasn't worth the money and danger. As noble as it is to have faith in divine protection, common sense still needs to prevail. I decided it was time for me to leave.

Our prime contractor leader might actually have liked me and the others. It was hard to tell. The management from my corporate group was so difficult to work with that they most likely gave him fits. This crusty southerner showed great restraint as he dealt with us on a daily basis during these confrontational events. He offered some friendly advice to me to be careful and protect myself from being a "fall guy" or scapegoat for the project.

Sad as it was to leave, I began to pack my gear. There were so many positives from the local people and the area up to this point: Insurgent activity had been quiet. The weather was still acceptable. The prime contractor was truly concerned about power production to the Iraqi electrical grid. We even watched several convoys of tractor trailers park their load of special cargo near our camp. Each of these huge cargo boxes were labeled in English and Arabic, "From the People of Kuwait to the People of Iraq." It was special goods for humanitarian relief from Kuwait. It was a changing climate, and it was exciting to be a witness of it.

Our security advisors were not allowed to discuss anything with me or the others dealing with the nightshift decision. Under their breath, they said they were sorry, but trump cards were used by higher authorities in their organization. All the Filipinos wanted to leave as well as the Scottish engineer. The two other Americans decided they would stay; they wanted the higher pay rates of Iraq work and felt it was worth the risk. They probably weren't alerting folks back home to as many details as the rest of us were. And they were optimistic that the security arrangement would change.

So, five of the seven of us departed. We were swiftly transported to the border by armored vehicle team at first daylight. All the way to the border drop, and even at the hotel in Kuwait, the Scottish engineer and I discussed how we particularly felt terrible at the way things had ended. In my mind, it was kind of the opposite of the "Return with Honor" principle. We didn't complete the task, and we left good and innocent people behind. But the working environment was just not acceptable to a majority of us, and we exercised our option to leave.

Our corporate people assured us there were replacements for us to keep the project progressing after our departure. Funny, though, that the local Iraqi plant workers and the US government certainly weren't found anywhere in this final equation.

The hotel stay in Kuwait City just wasn't fun. It was more like an overnight stay after a funeral. Flights were arranged, and we split up. As I waited in the room the evening before my flight, the phone rang. It was the other Scottish engineer from our sister project at Malik's plant. He was in camp using his cell phone. He said, "Mark, you are vindicated." Asking what he meant, he told me a roadside bomb had just narrowly missed the security teams coming in for work that evening at our project. It was close to the gate of the plant and was most likely targeted for them specifically. Everyone was unharmed, but they would be restricted from the plant for a while again. I thanked him for the update as we chit-chatted more, then hung up. There was nothing else to do but get on my knees and say a prayer for all of them. I was nearing the conclusion of my Iraq experience.

CHAPTER 11

It took time to adjust after arriving home. Taking in the fact that I was home again and the emotional uproar after the transport from one world to another was tumultuous. Stepping back into my world differed to my previous experience. Unlike the elated anticipation of returning that I had before, feelings of guilt for leaving swirled inside of me. As I listened to some talk radio within a day or two, a young woman called in to comment. She sounded sweet and basically a soccer mom type. I listened carefully as she calmly explained that maybe America and others should not intervene in faraway places. Her perception of the Iraqi people was of a society that desired death and destruction and were inherently disposed to breed hate and anger throughout the world. I was crushed. I was also dismayed at the manner in which this woman was swayed into her opinion. Media forces who focus so heavily on the price of liberty and not on the results had shaped her into believing a preconceived notion about Iraqi people. One by one, I thought about my friends in Iraq at that very instant during her comments. The entire exchange cut me to the very core of my soul. I felt helpless. Her discussion did not describe my loving and giving friends I had just spent a collective five months in Iraq with.

But the heartbreak of this episode was the relative ignorance in which this notion was formed. There was a tone of innocence as she spoke. The concept of an industrious and thriving people who love peace and abhor violence was nowhere in her dialogue. Only the reformulation of media soundbites, molding an opinion which by most standards would be considered prejudice. It occurred to me that there is a segment of our society that no longer took the time to reason out what we hear in today's media. I was frustrated at that concept of ignorance and stupidity.

I can only say that today I miss my Iraqi friends dearly, and I think about them every day. At first, I had to work hard to remember their names. Today, I cannot forget them nor will I ever be able to. I know of their personal goodness from my time with them, and I truly love them. Their countenance never did testify against them, and the love and respect between us was a two-way street. I actually miss being special and waving to strangers and children. That return receipt of the ice-breaking smile along with salutations from the heart is a special feeling. It is a reward that money and possessions cannot supplant.

To experience this love of strangers is an awesome weight. The true love of Christ should never find us confined within family, ethnic, or religious bounds. For us, it is to have charity toward all men as well as the household of faith (see D&C 121:45). It is undoubtedly a boundaryless principle that transcends culture, language, and national origin. I believe it is a principle that we will carry with us beyond the grave.

A familiar story goes this way. A man is beaten, robbed, and left for dead. Others pass by that are too busy or just don't want to get involved to offer assistance. One that is despised by these others offers aid. He even forfeits some of his own resources to aid the victim. Why would you not help him?

To give and to receive the strength of charity or the true love of Christ is a powerful force in the world. It was that tinge of a *Dances with Wolves*–flavored experience from the first trip that allowed me to withstand the dangers and completely immerse myself in the cultural exchange. To just live life tends to imply little growth. To experience life indicates a rich depth—and I experienced Iraq. Was it a happenchance series of events that I was privileged to experience?

Shortly after the September 11 attacks, a prominent US senator declared, "I'm not interested in changing the way I live. I'm interested in changing the way they live." Unfortunately, segments of our society demand changes to execute at accelerated paces, which can become unreasonable to achieve. Much of our lifestyle is built around that "want it now"–type attitude. Fast food restaurants dominate our culture and even offer drive-thru abilities, allowing us to never leave our vehicles. We have become so quick-conscious that we don't even slow down to describe our selected food items but merely recite a number to describe what menu order is our preference. It is truly a system of convenience and hurry. Do we watch too many movies that introduce us to characters, plots, and conclusions in a two-hour time span and further dull our senses to real time? The fear in our impatient society of today means we rarely take the time to patiently wait for progress like the Iraqi people. Because of them, they've changed the way I think, which can change the way I live. It doesn't alter my shopping habits to a great extent. And it doesn't change my vacation plans. The realization of the blessings we have, the freedoms, the prosperity—all become forefront in the thinking process now. And the change of life-style has been one for the better. What I learned was so much about humility, gratitude, hope, and faith in God.

I felt more comfortable with my Iraqi workers the first trip. The second trip should have been no different, but I just didn't get to work with the men. Iraqi men were basically the same on the second trip. So, what was the difference? Greed and self-interest should not be confused, but they are often separated by a thin, gray line. The fact that I had to deal predominately with my people changed things. It was that injection of corporate concerns, contract disputes, and corporate politics, as some call it.

Recovery time was needed again. My employer called shortly after I got home, and any conversation was pointless at that time. I was soured and needed time before thinking about another assignment anywhere. I didn't want a pound of flesh for the danger of the conditions of that assignment, I wanted a pound of flesh for them making it difficult for us because of their petty worries and dollar-driven motives. Never in my life have I been able to perform my job with such humble people and receive such personal satisfaction as I did in Iraq. And while none of us should be naïve and think that every project in Iraq is stacked with great local people, we should all be aware that the silent majority in Iraq and elsewhere in the world are the good people of the earth.

So, what is one to surmise from the conclusion to my experience? Greedy corporate management looking at the bottom line while a concerned prime contractor tries to expeditiously deliver a result? An inattentive security firm adjusting to the area? These situations are just the reality of the world we live in. Part of mortality is adapting to events and circumstances that just do not execute as planned. Life itself can be a twisty, gnarled path of unknowns for us to analyze, judge, and organize to the best of our ability while maintaining faithful and obedient attitudes throughout our time away from our Heavenly Father. How we adjust and plan our path can become an important educator to us in our eternal progression.

CONCLUSION

BY DAVID WEHLE, AUTHOR'S SON

In 2007, two years after the conclusion of his first trip, my father returned to Iraq. He planned to share all the many experiences he had in the latter half of this book, but it wasn't to be. As I go through the copious amounts of notes, journal entries, and photographs from his second trip, I mourn over the stories he never got to share. This five-month visit to the Al-Qudas power plant north of Baghdad is where my dad's love for the people only solidified, and it's what convinced him he needed to write a book to share with the world.

Here's what I can piece together from the various journal entries and letters he sent me while I was serving a Latter-day Saint mission: the task to bring electricity back to the Iraqi people was a resounding success! Multiple news agencies (including the *New York Times*), General Electric's public relations division, and even the news agency for the US Army covered the gradual but triumphant progress being made specifically at the Qudas power plant. When my dad arrived back in Iraq, word of mouth literally took over the region, with rumors being spread between the Iraqi people that Mr. Mark was actually back helping outside of Baghdad. One of his associates mentioned he had never heard of a single American man causing such a stir in a country before. A handful of his old friends from Basra were able to meet up with him at the new power plant, but the dangers of traveling across the countryside prevented any large reunions.

My brother Matthew took inspiration from our father's first trip and decided to help the school children in Iraq for his Eagle Project for the Boy Scouts of America. He coordinated the donation of thousands of school supplies to be sent to two schools near Baghdad for over 300 children. In an unusual twist for an Eagle Project, my dad was actually in Iraq to find the school supplies and make sure they were safely delivered. A local newspaper covered the event, with my brother saying, "I think this is a good way to help the children of Iraq who got stuck in the middle of everything. They're just children. I'm sure they know what's going on, but it's not their fault. And they don't have the things we take for granted."

A man named Jassim lived in the village where the school supplies were delivered, and he was also one of my dad's close friends and trusted workers at the Qudas power plant. They shed tears together, with my dad saying that "sweet, smiling faces were in abundance that day. Jassim told me how his heart was filled that day being present for this event." My dad told the interviewer that there is an Iraqi Arabic word pronounced "*bil-laf-eyah*" that means one is full and satisfied after a meal or clean and fresh after a shower or bath. "I can say that my heart was definitely '*bil-laf-eyah*' after seeing the pictures that Jassim, my true friend and hero, brought back for me and all of us to enjoy."

In another positive twist in the story, the second trip paid much better than the first one. My dad always made vague comments about how fortunate we were financially and how we would be able to pay off the house in record time. This proved to be a gigantic blessing since it alleviated so much financial stress from my mom after his untimely passing. My parents originally thought the extra money would help them prepare to serve missions earlier than they anticipated, and while the Lord was in the background protecting our family financially, it wasn't for the reasons we assumed. While we would've given anything to have our dad back with us, the idea that my mom was taken care of financially due to my dad's sacrifices in Iraq was a weight off our shoulders.

It still breaks my heart to know how many important stories my dad wanted to share from his second trip, and how he is now unable to. Only snippets remain in my memory: friendly Bible debates with an American Baptist named Wyatt. A sheep's neck sliced open in the desert with a bloody handprint imprinted on machinery for good luck. Sandstorms so thick it made the world look like the surface of Mars. Although my dad had a lot of fun sharing the visceral, bombastic stories, his short vignettes always came back to the same conclusion: he loved the people of Iraq, and they loved him.

I thought the best way to share a small part of his stories from Baghdad would be to compile the letters he wrote to me when I was a missionary in California. They've been edited for clarity and coherence. These were the stories and people that further shaped his time in Iraq, and I hope you see not only the love of a caring father to his children but also the love that a true disciple of Christ has toward his fellow man.

TRIP TO QUDAS
LETTERS FROM THE AUTHOR

September 2, 2007

Dear Elder David,

OK, I'm here again, I guess we're both doing missions. Mine for finances and yours for the gospel. I really think I can get some good gospel messages across in the process. Yesterday one of the Iraqi men eating lunch with us told everyone else to go back to the office while he and I talked about religious topics in the Dining Facility (DFAC). He is an Iraqi man that left Iraq years ago and went to London to live. He's back to help rebuild the country. We talked about the Godhead being three separate individuals and how Jesus is in the image of Heavenly Father. He said I was the first Christian that didn't seem confused about the Father, Son and Holy Ghost. He accepted my analogy of Jesus being like Heavenly Father, same as earthly sons are like their earthly fathers. The hang up for them (many Muslims) is a Koran verse that says, "I am God and I beget none, nor am I begotten" or something like that. I explained that I could not intellectually prove the divinity of Christ, but that was the job of the Holy Ghost, and he seemed ok with that. He had another piece of doctrine from the Koran he thought was a trump card, but one of the other Muslim guys disputed that with him and he agreed and changed his mind. This told me that people like him are open and the day might come when the Holy Ghost will convert people like him to the fact that Jesus is the Christ.

I'm at Camp Victory right outside Baghdad airport. It's a big Army Base and they have everything such as mail, shopping, good food, church services [LDS is listed as well as Catholic, Lutheran and non-denominational], probably a couple Army Units from Utah are here. Today is Sunday, but I'm going to a construction meeting in Amman Jordan and have to fly out today and will be back here Friday. They want me to go back to Qudas and help "rescue" the construction project from collapse. Basically, the project is "in the toilet" with regards to schedule, money and quality. I'm not going to have mail and shopping once I'm back at Qudas Power Plant. It will be email only when I get to Qudas next week!

Love, Dad

February 5, 2008

Dear Elder David,

As usual, another interesting round of events working with the guys. We always seem to get done with our business talk and drift over into the cultural stuff. Today alone I did the following . . . Learned about courtship and marriage in modern Iraqi Islamic society. Hussain explained how he met his wife and how both clans meet and give the "OK" then they can get engaged. Hussain said that men wear silver rings and women get gold rings . . . something to do with fertility and the Prophet Muhammad's teachings. A young worker named Yousef came in to clean the office and he's asking my help to find four lost uncles. Two were kidnapped and two others lost after they went looking for the first two in Fallujah. I have to contact the military Civil Affairs Team, and they will help.

Dr. Hamed came in today to say goodbye to me because his contract is over with the construction company. He's actually only about forty, and he teaches civil engineering at Baghdad University. His specialty is concrete mix design, and he's proven to be pretty good so far. He came in a couple days ago, and after the business talk was over, he wanted to know about his medical treatment for his knees, which are giving out. He thinks he needs a better checkout somehow with modern equipment. His situation brought to mind the situation with another Mohammad a year ago whose son needed some heart work and I emailed pictures of the x-ray to Jonathan's Dr. in Richmond and Dr. Albrecht helped with the diagnosis.

Today was great . . . we stopped talking business and started getting into why I was not "American." They have a stereotype about Americans based on movies, and I had to explain why "my Christianity" was different. They always guess Catholic cause that's all they know and then I tell them "Mormon" (Mom hates that . . . but how do you elaborate LDS Church to Muslims?). So, I explain that our Church is worldwide, and they want to know why it is so close to Islam . . . they know the no smoking, no alcohol thing. I tell them about how we do our prayers and family prayer. They were surprised that prayers are (supposed to be . . . it's in D&C) three times a day. Then I get to explain why we are different, and I draw a diagram on the whiteboard and kind of explain what the Christian world consists of. Europe divided and basically loyal to Catholic or Protestant, England forming the Church of England (Episcopal) because King Henry the Eighth wanted to get a divorce. But America has so many splits from there I explain, and there is much choice. And I mention that a prophet might be for a specific people, and they nod their heads. They're moderates! You see it! These people aren't hardcore "Muhammad is the last Prophet" type thinkers. Then I get to explain about Utah because they ask where are these people in the USA, and I explain about the migration and our prophet, and they even ask his name and I get to say "Joseph Smith" and how we have more scriptures than other Christians. So, I left a commitment that before we part ways when the project is over, I will explain fully.

So, what is the difference with their ability to convert and the Jews? It's always going to be the Spirit. That's what the scriptures tell us . . . the Spirit will be the converting factor. Right now, I guess a lot of the Muslim world is stuck on the pride of being Abraham's seed. OK . . . I'm going to go for now. Do you like these letters?

More Later,

Love, Dad

February 8, 2008

Dear Elder David,

Another fantastic round of events since my last letter two or three days ago. The Minister of Electricity showed up, and I had already guessed what was going on. One of the similar turbine units in operation has crashed out and the Iraqi plant manager does not want to admit that it needs a major overhaul. So, the minister shows up and wants to see this for himself. It was an amazing show of force when the minister arrived. Sirens, helicopters, army men with lots of guns surrounding him, armored Jeeps and armored cars, all coming toward us as we were looking at the turbines under construction. One of our British security guards starts walking toward the minister's armed men, and we start to warn our guy to stop and let them come to us. So, we wait, and he comes to us, and we get to meet him, and I get to discuss the plant issues and the construction. He asked if we would get done by June, and I basically said no. Then he asked Nasir when he thinks he'll get done . . . Nasir is the site manager for the Iraqi construction company that the Corps of Engineers hired to do this job. So, Nasir stumbles around and tells him June, and I don't say a word . . . a true "common sense" event for me.

Then, I spend the rest of the day on humanitarian issues . . . a man named Hayder works for the MoE (Ministry of Electricity) and wants another job working for the Corps of Engineers or anybody in the power business. It is a new thing for Iraqis to prepare a CV (European word for a resume). So, Hayder hands me this CV, and it is pathetic . . . I make him get more details in it before I review it again and begin to help him touch it up. The MS Word document is in English, but it's goofed up because of the Arabic right to left formatting and stuff, and I have to figure out how to edit it without the cursor popping all over the place like chaos.

Then, the young guy Yousef who cleans the office trailer comes in, and we struggle through some conversation and find out that he has four uncles that are missing. Two were working in Fallujah on a US government job, and they were kidnapped. So, two more uncles went looking for them about a month later, and now they are missing. So, Yousef brings pictures, and I'm making a short, written history to send out to the Army unit to help locate the people. Can you imagine that Uncle Kurt goes missing and me and Uncle Greg and Shad team up to go find him and we're missing too? Why do we have it so made in America? Are we spoiled and don't realize our own blessings?

Later Dr. Hamad comes in with his x-ray in hand and I become the doctor. I need to find a doctor in the US who will look at the picture and tell me what kind of treatment he needs for his knees. Do you know any doctors in the mission? Maybe Doctors without Borders will do it? But how do you turn these people away like Yousef and Hamad? Is part of my service here in Iraq to spread cheer, present a smiling face, and offer another glimpse of Americans? There is nothing but humility in these people. Today one of the (many) Mohammad's took some pictures of me, and I joked that "Was this for the militia?" He chuckled and said, "Mr. Mark, you are so safe here among us . . . we would never let anything happen to you. You are in OUR

Green Zone." It's hard to describe how this conversation made me feel. I really think the bulk of these people would take a bullet in defense of us Americans that are here helping.

So, I'm a missing persons location center, an employment specialist, a doctor, a missionary, and a power plant engineer. I really wonder if I could ever come back here as an old man like Brother Whitesides and teach the gospel? There seems to be so much of a connection with the Holy Land and Babylon that it boggles my mind. Do you know that the Urim and Thummin that Joseph Smith used to translate the Book of Mormon came from the Jaredites who came from the Tower of Babel? Basically, less than fifty miles from me. Do you know some of the men still call me "Abu-David?" It is another form of addressing men and it means "father of David."

OK . . . well we're making progress. Another good development is I'm getting to hire a couple of the Basra boys to come up here and work with us. So, I'm excited to be re-united and hang out with friends from my first trip here in 2004. Mom's even starting to get after me about the book and that's one of my strategies for writing these letters to you . . . it's almost like a journal and when I reread these letters after you're home, it will jar my memory.

Love, Dad

February 26, 2008

Dear Elder David,

I'm doing a good job, and everybody likes me . . . I'm a celebrity here in the plant. To be honest, it's just that I say "Hello" and try to smile everywhere I go out on the project. There are 300 people on the job, and it can be a little nerve-wracking being the leader and one of only three Americans. Most all of them know me and say "Hello" when they see me.

Hussain and I had a spiritual experience before Christmas when he wanted to know why I was different. I said it was my religion and what was in a person's heart, and I got a little choked up and felt the spirit at that moment. Hussain felt something.

Kareem saw my elbows awhile back and bought me some special soap the other day that he told me how to use. I was to use the phrase "Bissem Allah al-rah-mon al rah-heem," which means something like "The Most Gracious God and Dispenser of Grace" and it is one of the ways they ask for a health blessing while using the soap. So, think about it . . . I'm a High Priest in the true Church and children of Ishmael are giving me a blessing in the best manner they know how! I think this is all very historic somehow, but we just don't realize it.

I'm doing missionary work with Paul. He had a nasty divorce a few years ago and I talk about how marriage can be a great thing if it's done proper. I explained the plan of salvation and he asks a question every so often. Just planting seeds . . . that's all we can do sometimes. Wyatt is a Southern Baptist, and he listens and I'm not sure what he thinks sometimes. He's kind of a simple guy. It's scary, but to me I would want to make sure that the Church isn't true if I were concerned about Christ. When people don't inquire, I think they are those that are "fooled by the craftiness of Satan" and they're not the "sheep." The Lord's sheep hear His voice. Not that they're the goats, they just don't hear His voice for some reason. There is some relationship with the pre-earth life with all this I believe.

OK . . . I'm getting tired. The laptop is good, and Windows Vista stinks. I'm going to Amman Jordan at the end of this week, and I probably won't have time to write anymore until after the first weekend in March when I'm back here.

Love you, Abu-David (that's my Arabic name)

March 16, 2008

Dear Elder David,

I have a new Iraqi American guy with me that works for the same company I do. He lived out near Las Vegas and his dentist was LDS and some other friends. He knows a lot about the Church but not some of the details and I've been explaining them to him . . . "*shoy-ya, shoy-ya*" (little by little). He has noticed in America the strong reaction from Christians when they are confronted about Mormonism. And he is impressed by many of the similarities with Islam, and he even said the other day that maybe Joseph Smith studied Islam or something to get some of the rules into the Mormon faith. I said, "Maybe they are both from God?" That got him thinking! He has helped so much with the language barrier at work. We have a good relationship.

I had another missionary experience with a Scottish guy that is one of our guards here at the site. Last night I went outside to talk to some of the guys, and I heard bagpipes playing! I found out that the Scotsman had brought his bagpipes and was in a bomb shelter for privacy and was playing away! It was awesome! The sound and the harmony were overwhelming . . . but what he was playing took my breath away and I had to step back to get my composure. He was playing Hymn 27 "Praise to the Man" . . . it is a famous Scottish folk song called "Scotland the Brave" and the music resonated throughout my body. I felt the Spirit and my gratitude for the mission of Joseph Smith and the strength of the Church in our current day. I got to discuss Church history with him as I explained that the tune is one of our most revered hymns in the Church. He wants a copy of the hymn in an .mp3 format or something to listen to. I'd like to get him something a little more contemporary instead of the Mormon Tabernacle stuff, or maybe a couple different renditions of it . . . any suggestions? Do you know any versions with bagpipes?

Another development on the missionary work of Iraq that I get a small part in . . . the new officer who is in charge of our project might be LDS. I have to double check this, but I found this out from Hussain and Kareem who are the Iraqi guys that work for us. Now how did they find this out? These Iraqi local guys are quite aware of my "different" faith of Christianity, and they look for it! They start trying to find out what "type" of Christians the Americans are. This was unheard of a few years ago. They just figured that the Pope was our man and all the Christians followed him. I get goosebumps thinking of teaching the gospel to some Christian Iraqis at some point in the future. Could you imagine the people lined up for baptism? Humble people that are not tainted by corrupted religion and thirsting for the truth . . . the Spirit touching them as they committed themselves into the waters of baptism. Just as in the early days of the Church when thousands came to hear the Elders and joined the Church. I can see where Joseph Smith's name would be had amongst ALL nations of the earth in the future! Maybe your lifetime? Maybe your children will serve a mission in the Middle East?

Love you much and praying for you always,

Love, Dad

March 24, 2008

Dear Elder David,

Hope you got my last letter quickly. It's been a good week. First the good news that I need your help with. One of the security guards is from Fiji and we got talking about the Church and he wants to get baptized! I thought you could help by getting me a Book of Mormon in Fijian as soon as possible, then pack it up and send it to me in the US mail at the Camp Cooke address. I start getting goose bumps thinking about baptizing him in Iraq and having all my Muslim friends watch and feel the Spirit, but that will never happen. There are rules about religious activity, so all I can do is quietly give him a Book of Mormon in his native language and help him prepare for baptism for when he goes home on leave in about ten months. He is such a humble spirit . . . he goes by "Rus," but I think his Fijian name is more difficult to pronounce.

We have a weekly meeting with the Iraqi government power plant owners, and I notice that they always serve the drink called "Hummel" to us instead of "Chii." Hummel is a lemon-type hot drink and Chii is the standard hot drink that all Iraqis' love and it is a very strong tea. Nasir, the Iraqi company manager of my project, explained to everyone my religious restrictions about Word of Wisdom doctrine. I'm kind of honored that they respect me so much and go out of their way to accommodate me.

The new guy, Tarik, who's from Iraq but is an American, is working out great. He's a Shia Muslim and he keeps asking questions about the Church. He just sees a lot of similarities and he thinks the LDS Church is the most organized of all the Christian religions in America. A day hardly goes by without us talking about our religions. The other guy in the office is a southern Baptist, but he's not hard-core and annoying. I think I kind of blew him away yesterday when he asked about how the LDS explained the polygamy and the Bible scripture about the bishop having "one wife" as it's written in the Bible somewhere. I said, well we believe in revelation and then I explained the story in the Bible about Jesus and Peter and the Rock of Revelation (Matt. 16:18). He just didn't have anything to say. So, I have to use intellect to a certain degree, then let the Spirit do the rest if that time ever comes for him to question his faith and look at ours.

Bad news now . . . the new Army guy in charge of us is a Utah inactive LDS and he smokes and drinks the Chii. So, I told him that I spent months indoctrinating the Muslim guys on what LDS is about and our strictness, and he'd have to pay attention to himself now. But how did I find out he was LDS? Well, the Iraqi guys asked him! Yes, they have been interested in how many Americans are a part of this religion, and they snooped out the Colonel's faith and came back and told me! It might be good that the guys see an inactive member and know that we have "lost sheep" just like any others and that I'm not angry with him but just disappointed. I told Mom about it on the phone, and she was pretty upset that someone like him would even declare himself LDS . . . he should just stay in the closet about this. I'll have to pray about it and scheme some sort of damage control as it comes up. The subject came up with

Tarik and I told him it was my "duty" as it is possible to get him back into the proper guidelines of behavior of the Church. I think Tarik was a little stunned at the answer and scared I was going to make a scene or something. Then I explained things like this are done gently with love and with proper timing.

Yesterday was Easter and lots of the Iraqi men came by the office to give best wishes and brought food and junk food for me. Ehmad (E-Mod) is a Kurdish and Baghdad man, and he came by to explain that Muslims believe that Asis (Jesus) was removed from the cross by God and continued to live on the earth until he was taken back to heaven. He said that Islam teaches that Jesus will return in the future and rule the earth for one thousand years . . . wow, I didn't know that Islam teaches this.

I keep thinking about the book and go back and forth in my mind if it's a stupid thing or not. Maybe I should just do it and it will be for the Wehle posterity. Today an Iraqi man gave me an empty drug package for blood pressure treatment that his wife needs. He said the Iraqi medicine is a low quality and asked for my help. It is so humbling! They ask me for humanitarian needs, they ask me for my advice, they ask me about my faith, they ask about my family, they smile at me, they wave at me, they bring me food, they never overstep the bounds of decency or ask for things of comfort and convenience . . . only things of need and things we take for granted. Fadhil is one of the men I know from last year here at Qudas . . . he just asked for help getting quality baby food for his little boy who has some form of jaundice or something. I get jealous thinking of who will be the first Church member to baptize an Iraqi citizen and when will that be? Could it be me in later years? Is this why I'm here . . . to plant seeds? Most of the time all I can give them is a smile and a wave . . . but to them that is enough. It's almost to the point where I can't bear the thought of working with rough-cut Americans with their trivial drama in the future. This is the experience of a lifetime and cannot be replaced. I do cherish everyday here and despite the danger I feel the Lord is looking out for me and has a purpose for me here . . . even if it is just to offer a smile and a wave.

Love you, Dad

April 8, 2008

Dear Elder David,

We had a lockdown week before last while they had some Iraqi Army stand-off in Basra with the militia. There were riots in Baghdad, and bombs were going off in the distance. We had two mortars land near the plant, and they went off with a pretty big thud. The security guys whisked us out of there pretty quickly and into the armored vehicles then back to the camp. The captain of the guard of the power plant had his thirteen-year-old son killed and his eight-year-old daughter died from injuries in the fighting. There's a chance that he could be bitter and try to hurt us here at the plant, so we have to wait and see. The military folks didn't respond quite like we thought they would to investigate how this man feels, but we have to give them more time still.

Hussain, one of the Iraqi men that works for us, and many of the other guys have explained how the militia works in Iraq. Basically, all of them have no formal education and no work skills. So, they join the militia for income and are easily swayed by the militia leadership. If there were more work available, they wouldn't join, and they would go to their jobs and earn money, raise families, and stay busy. It sure seems that the scriptures are correct about idleness and wickedness going hand in hand.

Had another hair-raising experience talking about Joseph Smith to Tarik the Iraqi-American guy here with me. He asked the questions, so I answered. I had to explain that Joseph is a prophet and that today we are led by a succession of prophets. He seemed pretty much okay about this and then even asked if I had any religious books and so forth, and he let me know he was always willing to read religious literature for his own self benefit. On Saturday the fifth, some very humble Iraqi men came into the office, and I could feel their humble and pure hearts as we discussed about doing business with their little struggling company. They supply the cement for the job. I think one was a Christian because I just felt something about him .. . he looked a little like Uncle Richard. They were just pure people and something very good and pure about them . . . . I can't explain it. I wish I could just jump up and start talking Church doctrine with them.

But I have a real historic event to think about. I was listening to General Conference first session live on the internet, but it kicked off for a second. When I got it back, they were sustaining the General Authorities and were having PH and RS and Youth stand separately as a group and sustain or oppose the new First Presidency and GA's. Then they said "All members gathered everywhere" or something like that . . . so I stood up here in my room and held my hand up with the entire Church, at the same time, and sustained the new prophet from Iraq. Now there might be military men doing this here also, but how many are on non-military bases and standing on sovereign Iraqi soil? So, I believe I am the first member to sustain a true prophet in this dispensation on pure sovereign Iraqi soil (or actually in the ancient land of Babylon). Or possibly the first person to ever sustain a true prophet in the ancient land of Babylon since the Jewish captivity of the Old Testament times or possibly ever. Maybe we should put that in Mormon Reader as a trivia fact?

Gordon the Scottish guy played his bagpipes at night in the camp. All the Iraq guys who were off work came to listen and got fired up and started doing their native dances around Gordon as they got all charged up with the music. At one point a couple of the on-duty guards walked by with their machine guns and joined in the dancing . . . they were dancing around in a circle holding hands all singing excitedly in Arabic and waving their guns up and down in the air. They weren't firing the guns or anything, but it is still quite the scary scene . . . like wild, *Lord of the Flies*-type action. Gordon and I were laughing because we realized if anybody from our world ever saw that scene they would probably pass out and die from fear. As usual, I jumped in right with them at the peak of the frenzy and had a ton of fun with all these guys. Gordon made the comment that "Music is the International language" . . . how true. For several days after, all the guys would excitedly say something to me about what fun that was dancing around Gordon that evening.

I went to Jassim's house and visited his family (they have two young daughters). I am probably one of a very few Americans that have gotten to go inside an Iraqi family household and eat, talk, and enjoy some time with their children. They taught me an Iraqi game that I've forgotten already... sort of like a tic-tac-toe type thing. In return I showed them . . . what else . . . tic-tac-toe, and I'm sure they've forgotten it already also. There's a girl named Nada just like your cousin. She also knows she's kind of my favorite due to her name. She always runs up and gives me a hug when she sees me. The TV and DVD is relatively a new thing for Iraqi households. Jassim has money due to his contracts with our man camp and the work he does with the construction project I'm working on, so he can afford these luxuries. Saddam outlawed satellite TV but the elite were able to get permission and have nice cars, TV, cell phones, etc.

A favorite experience that deals with Jassim's kinfolk was last year when our construction equipment man was kidnapped by militia. His name is Mahmoud, and I included him in my prayers when I heard the news. He escaped a few days later and I told him I was saying prayers for him, and he appreciated it. Today every time I see Mahmoud after a few days of him being away, we greet each other in the traditional Iraqi style of several cheek-to-cheek kisses. I didn't know that Mahmoud is from the village of Tarmiya (Matt's Eagle Project school), or that he is Jassim's cousin. Today they all say that Mr. Mark owns the Tarmiya militia . . . school supplies, concern for their citizens, and all the small things I've been able to do have made me a popular person in the village households of Tarmiya.

Hope you enjoy the pics and the stories . . . write me a letter soon. Love you Son, I hope I spent enough time doing spiritual things with you during the years.

Love, Dad

April 16, 2008

Elder David,

I forgot that you never got the story on Matt's Eagle Scout Project conclusion. Here's the story... we start with the hero... Jassim. I had to locate all the boxes and get them to the Qudas Power Plant. I started asking folks right after I got there on September 14th. My good friend Jassim who works at the plant helping us with the generators and the water came to the rescue. We found out that most of the boxes went to South Baghdad power plant. Before the "Troop Surge," Jassim would not have even considered making a trip like this across town... this time would be no problem.

We had to store all the items at the camp in an air-conditioned room... it was so hot that we could smell the crayons melting. There were bunches of boxes and many different types of supplies donated. People were generous and Matt did a good job with the money he used to buy the supplies and we had a large variety.

It was a good haul and all safely stored for now. Ramadan was coming up and school wouldn't be starting until after the month of Ramadan. Jassim and I tried to divide up the goods for each child but it was an overwhelming task... we ended up laughing about it that we even tried to do this, so we gave up and quit for the time. We needed to give it some thought.

Jassim had to play with the A/C a little and stick some bare wires into a 220-volt socket to get a good power contact. I fussed at him while he was doing this, and his thought process in regards to this was that God will protect him. Because he was engaged in a righteous cause such as this, he feels God will protect him from harm. This is their culture mentality and is a typical example of their faith-based life. I reminded him that God still wants us to use our intellect and exercise sound judgement when near danger. He agreed and took precautions while I gritted my teeth until he was done. We got the A/C working fine.

Jassim and I both came to the same conclusion a few days later… we would just do a clean-up of the boxes and try to separate the bulk of it and turn it over to the school somehow. But Jassim had a unique perspective when he explained to me his thoughts about it…

Mohee is the man who we arranged the school supplies project with to start with. He works for Reed Security at the man camp… his brother is a Sheik or is like one of the Town Elders of the Tarmiya Village. Jassim and I consider Mohee a religious man and very trustworthy. Ali-Baba is a big concern here so something valuable like these supplies needed a trusted person to help. We both came to the same conclusion that we'll just have Mohee tell us how to proceed. We later found out that another of Mohee's brothers and a sister-in-law worked at the school, so it was a great choice.

So, we cleaned it all up and replaced the boxes with good ones and Jassim scheduled delivery for the first or second day of school. I tried to get Jassim to take money but he said "No, you help my people, I help you."

Jassim wanted me to give a few bags of goodies to his girls and some of the local kids that lived on the plant and went to school in a different village. The driver stopped by and Jassim snapped a picture of me with his youngest girl on their way home from school.

The head of the village school system and his assistant met Jassim and anxiously helped with the unloading. These men marveled at the generosity that unknown Americans would show by providing much needed items for their small village school system. Crayons, colored pencils, water color paints, finger paints, construction paper, pencils and sharpeners, pens, art supplies, modeling clay, glue, scissors, notebooks, coloring books, small carry pouches, stickers, picture books, stamps and stamp pads, small toddler toys, jump ropes, and even girls hair ribbons were among the cornucopia of items that came pouring in from loving families anxious to respond to Matthew's call for donations.

The day came and the obedient youngsters all stood up as tradition when the School Headmaster and village leaders entered the classroom. Items were given out as sweet faces and smiles were found in abundance that day. Jassim got my pictures and told me how his heart was filled that day being present for this event.

Hope this was a good letter for you . . .

Love, Dad

April 28, 2008

Elder David,

I'm always late doing this letter, but I get more action into it when more time goes by. So, these last two weeks have been interesting. I also have a challenge at hand with the South Carolina Baptist guy, Wyatt, and Tarik the Iraq-American. But I will say this about Tarik . . . when he asks me a question about Christian doctrine and he wants to know the Mormon perspective, he always seems satisfied or agrees to disagree, but he is always interested in how we know so much about Abraham and God's covenant and such. Apparently, it's more than Islam has, and it gets him to wonder. The other day he started looking at the Book of Mormon in Arabic here in my room and asking more questions, then he said "Okay, let's stop before you convert me!" That was an unexpected statement from him . . . so we did change the topic.

But we come into the office in the camp away from the job site and we start getting into these philosophical discussions. Seems that Wyatt starts them, and it feels like Wyatt wants to prove Tarik wrong or something or find fault with the Koran compared to his Baptist beliefs. But Wyatt has a good heart and don't misunderstand that he's mean-spirited or anything . . . he just believes passionately about his faith. But I always wonder to myself . . . why doesn't a Bible person want to know more about Joseph Smith? Or why wouldn't they want to "make sure" that the Book of Mormon ISN'T true and study it out to ease their conscience? What is it that threatens them and why do they resist? Is it something to do with the pre-existence?

Why did I recognize it and the Spirit testified to me that it was true? I don't get it. Did you pay attention to Elder Oaks' talk about testimony at General Conference? It's spiritual witness, not intellectual. So, we have these intellectual exchanges that end up wearing me out, and I don't want to participate. And even Tarik gets so philosophical that I lose interest. So, I can sum up the world problems with this simple conclusion . . . "Let the works of God be made manifest." That's the Savior's teaching in response to "Who sinned, this man or his parents?" I guess that things happen so that the plan of salvation can carry forth, and each of us is responsible to act accordingly in the circumstances that find ourselves put in. It all still boils down to personal accountability and the light of Christ in our lives.

So, from our talks here in the camp I've learned a few things about Islamic thought. They find great personal anguish when we try to imagine the nature of God and try to attach an image of Him with that. It's almost to the point of blasphemy to them. So, when we say you've seen the Father because we've seen the Son, they can't accept that. They don't care about any degree of salvation . . . they accept anything they get, so there's no striving for the higher, just minimize the risks of not getting the best they're going to be given. Kind of confusing, eh? But I realized that they are full of teachings or "law" from commentary on the Koran. So, I always ask if a thought or doctrine is Koran or from "commentary" and a lot is from commentary over the years.

We had another sandstorm the other day that was the most orange I've seen yet. The picture is pretty wild. It's like it is snowing or something except it's dusty. I can't believe it is like this out here. Some of the guys get eye infections and such from this, and I always want to just take a shower and hide out in my room. It's kind of like a cloudy day all day and the sun doesn't shine and it's actually cooler outside with wind.

I've been going nut case looking at all the rocks on the ground as I walk throughout the site. I keep thinking about the Brother of Jared having the Lord touch the stones for light in the ships. Those stones became the Urim and Thummim that were buried with the plates in Cumorrah. Maybe they looked like these rocks except the scriptures say they were like glass. These rocks are smooth and Burgundy in color. I find some green ones every so often. The smooth comes from water erosion, this land was the land of many waters around that time.

More next time.

Love you, Dad

May 7, 2008

Elder David,

Well, Mohammed One from Basra is up here now to work. He got here a few days ago, and we had a big extended hug and shed tears. He said that the trip up was no problem from Basra to Baghdad . . . people were out in the streets and children playing soccer all over. He wasn't nervous during the trip. I worry that the Iraqi company might not treat him right and want him to know that he doesn't have to stay if it gets bad working for these guys. He's good about that and says I'm still his "teacher" and he'll do what's right if he has to make a decision.

All the Iraqi men in the Civil Department had a small feast with us today. I remember they told me they were going to do this about a week ago, and I forgot which day it was. But last night I started to do my fast and committed myself to be successful for twenty-four hours, then at work the men told me today was the day for the eating. They brought "Dolma," which is like dirty rice stuffed into grape leaves or small onions or small eggplants then kind of steamed in a big pot. It has a very slight vinegar taste and takes a lot of work to prepare. So, I didn't even consider telling them I was trying to do a good fast this month and they were making me blow it! I skipped lunch and sat in my room here and listened to General Conference talks on my iPod and waited to get back to work at about 1 p.m. then eat with the men. So, I just prayed for the Lord to forgive me for a bad fast and realized I was about four or five hours from a successful twenty-four-hour fast. Maybe not that bad and better than some months where I didn't do it at all.

I learned some interesting Wyatt the Baptist stuff recently. He was assigned at a small government power plant in Idaho named Palisades near Idaho Falls some years ago. He must have had some LDS interaction there to some extent and learned of the doctrine. You know I just have to wonder why someone rejects the idea of a prophet and revelation? And the idea of making a law unto themselves just comes to mind. But he is a good guy with a good heart . . . so why is it that someone like me joins the Church, and a good person like him just doesn't? Am I casting my pearls before swine when I get into discussions with him? Why do I recognize it and he doesn't? Why does he get so intellectual about the whole thing? Does he need a sign to believe? The whole thing is weird. The Elders in Guam taught me that the Lord's sheep hear His voice . . . and I did! I heard it loud and clear!

Dr. Hamad came in this week to see how we were doing. He was the consultant for making the concrete mixture back in October for the foundations, and he works at Baghdad University. He says that the students are distracted because of the violence of the last few years and he's hoping for progress in this area. Last time he was here a few weeks ago, I asked how his family was doing and he said his wife was living with her mother and there were some problems. So, this time I asked again, and he leveled with me that he had some problems and like almost hears voices in his head or something like that, and he wishes that the Americans or British could "implant" something to make him right. It's all kind of weird. He takes some meds and talks to a psychiatrist.

So, I waited until it got kind of empty in the office, and I discussed spiritual matters with him and drew a circle on the whiteboard then made like a math problem out of it. By putting arrows pushing on the outside of the circle to make it collapse, I explained that these are the opposing forces of life . . . anger, pain, hate, hunger, fear, etc. Then I put opposite arrows on the inside of the circle pushing against the outside ones, and I assigned an opposite force like forgiveness, joy, love, food, courage, etc., and said these are some of the forces of life and it is our job to balance them throughout our life because this is the test. If we balanced them and kept the circle round, then we would have joy despite adversity. He agreed, and we discussed that having a strong family is the backbone and root of a strong nation. I got that doctrine from the Proclamation on the Family. So, I explained that regardless of what things he thinks his wife has done wrong, he needs to just forgive her and forget about it and start over and take charge of his family . . . they have a little boy about two years old. And I think he's going to do it or at least I got him thinking about it in a different manner. I had to explain more to him about the man and the women being as "one" and there was divine purpose in him and her discussing innermost thoughts together and how older couples know each other so well after many years because of this. I can't forget the talk by Elder Oaks about good, better, best . . . if you can affect and improve a life, that's best.

Kareem is superstitious about me collecting the rocks that I showed you in the last letter, so I have to hide them from him. It's like they believe the spirits of the "jinn" are imprisoned in the rocks and he believes that bad things can happen to us because of the rocks being around. The jinn is where the genies (in the lamp that you rub and make a wish) folklore comes from and I think it's something to do with stories from the Quran.

We sat down the other day with the guys, and they admitted that they judged Americans on what they see on TV from the American movies. It kind of disturbs us but at least we can help overcome a stereotype. We talked about the Iraq nation history before Islam and the guys said there are many books written about history at the Tower of Babel times and before. They said they didn't like Nebuchadnezzar for a certain reason, and I have to find out why they said that again.

Work is still slow and still no sign of picking up speed. They all quit work at about 3 p.m. and nothing gets done. We got inside news that the Iraq government crackdown on militias is working. It's actually a strategic move they made with the Americans doing some road blocking, and the Iraqi forces moving in and killing off any fighters that opposed them. There are so many military-age youth without jobs and so much hanging around, it's easy to see why they join militias to make money. It's not right to judge them eternally, but an intermediate judgement would tell me that their choices put them at risk of getting killed at an early age.

I talked with the Minister of Electricity a couple months ago. It's pretty awesome that he stopped, and I got to share my thoughts with him. He seemed like a good man but with heavy responsibility. His suit probably cost more than your whole mission. More later . . .

Love ya, Dad

June 1, 2008

Elder David,

Late again . . . aren't I excused because I talked to you on Mother's Day? But as always, good stuff, I hope. Work drama first. Wyatt is gone and Paul is back. So, no more intellectual talks in "The Room" down in the camp anymore. At one point we were anxious to go back to camp and have these deep discussions in the evenings. Then I started to get quiet a few times . . . it all wore me out. They started to notice, and my answer came out as to why I was quiet. I told them to me it was interesting to observe a Baptist defending his faith and explaining the plan of salvation to a non-Christian. It was the tables turned for once and not me defending my faith to another Christian who believes differently. I can say that the Wyatt Baptist plan of salvation is a "how I see it type of thing" and open to individual interpretation. Thank goodness for revelation and that we have the plan of salvation and all we need to know for our own benefit. There are some concepts in the PoS that I never thought about, but because of revelation and the testimony of the Holy Ghost I now have that knowledge and I now believe those concepts.

The Baghdad company is having a labor dispute and I end up in the middle of the two parties. Adnan is one of the engineers for the Civil Department . . . he is very small, and we call him "Yoda" behind his back. I was in his office the other day with all his staff there and we were discussing this labor "drama" and they explained their issues. They all drive together, and it is a long drive with danger, checkpoints, etc. Hade, Emad, Salim,

Ahmed, and Adnan all together. Adnan drives the vehicle. I couldn't help making a joke about Adnan being so small and being the driver that maybe nobody can see him . . . we all roared in laughter, and I went over to Adnan while we were ripping up and grabbed his hand for a shake, then pulled him in for a bear hug so he knows we love him. He knows and he laughed right with us, and we all felt the good feelings we have for each other.

There are other problems too with many of the guys not getting paid on time. I stood out there with about ten or twelve mad welders listening with them complain about pay issues and Hussain was discussing with them the issues about the pay. Man . . . I was thinking that the world really is guided by the Light of Christ cause these guys should have grabbed me and strung me up for a hanging. There tends to be this attitude from Army folks that issues like these don't matter . . . yes, they matter, and the good name of the US government is at stake if we don't follow up and ensure that the contractor is paying the people on-time. But there are issues with that too and I fully understand. But people tend to suppose that because it's written on a contract that all is well, and the human feeling and morale is not a factor in success or motivation. I really think Mom would faint if she saw some of the situations I go through here dealing with the people day after day. An update to this pay thing . . . they got their pay a few days ago and the big mean guy (Mustafa the welder) came over and shook my hand so hard I thought he might break it. So there always seems to be a good story behind the bad ones.

Nasir came in the day before to discuss this drama and him and Adnan got into it in our office. They speak guttural and rough with emphasis on words unlike what we do in English. Me and Paul didn't have a clue. It got quiet suddenly and I said to Nasir "Shineau?" which means "What?" Nasir replied "Nothing!" and he excused himself and they all filed out of the office. Paul and I just couldn't hold it back as they shut the door on the way out . . . we cracked up, tears coming out of our eyes. I had to go over to Nasir later and make sure he wasn't offended if he heard us laughing. As I explained our laughter to Nasir he started laughing too at how the whole thing must have looked to me and Paul. Someone (Emad) said there might be some Saddam connection with Nasir's family in the past. I said, "Well, you have to get a fresh start here, just like Germany did." Emad said, "Yes, but we're still at the beginning." So, they do realize this is for their children, and that they have to heal from the brutal years of the past.

Watching the whole labor and management thing going on I have seen firsthand how they argue in the culture . . . they seem rather fierce on their opinion, then when it's all over they come back with forgiveness with a gift offering and they clean the slate. This happened with Jassim and a guard here in the camp . . . and it got into a fist getting thrown. Then the apologies and gift exchange and all was cleared and no grudges. Today Jassim and the guard are bonded even tighter now, and I suspect it's because of the manner in which they reconcile like this.

Mohammed One is doing great. I am sneaking him into GE, and he will be a GE man for the job. I guess we Americans have cronyism also . . . I just intervened with this GE thing and I am guilty! Maybe we do it for more than money . . . maybe we do it for perfection of the work, for max profits, for friendship? I don't know. I was worried that he was going to be lonely and displeased with the assignment. But now all I was thinking about for him in my mind is starting to come to pass. Maybe the Lord is using him to bring about great things for him and his people in the future and I'm a tool to assist. Mohammed called me tonight on the cell phone and needed some info and I'm going to help. He asks why I am helping him so much and I told him that I just don't know, he considers me his brother beyond a doubt and says I help him "like his Father."

I had to go into the Baghdad Company mechanical guys office today and make sure all this drama isn't flowing over to them yet. But I was late, their GE man was canned and I'm afraid Mohammed One being put in his place could cause hard feelings . . . I wonder who knows all the CIA stuff I do behind the scenes?

I am really getting hyper about going home for the four-week break. I might be leaving tomorrow. I'll let you know how home is doing and how Cherie is doing at Riverside. More later.

Love, Dad

An Excerpt from Elder Matthew Wehle's Missionary Journal

Written on June 28 and 29, 2010

I truly don't have words to describe what I'm going through right now or how I feel. Today, at around 12 in the afternoon, my father passed away… My heart aches more than it ever has in my entire life. I've never felt more despair in my entire life. Knowing that my father has passed away today is still setting in. We were having Zone Conference at the time. Cherie sent me a text to our phone and I got it half-way through the conference. She just said that Dad had a heart attack. So, I walked up to the Mission President and told him about the text I had just received. He took me into a room outside the chapel and told me my father had just passed away. He gave me a blessing. Then the Assistants to the President came in with me while the Zone Conference was still going. Then I got to call home. Mom was about to leave for Georgia because that's where my father was when it happened. Jonathan was with Dad on this work trip too.

The Mission President gave me many words of counsel. He asked me if I knew where my father was, I said, "Paradise." Something he told me that I will never forget was this: "Elder

Wehle, he made it, he's a god. His calling and election was made sure today." The Mission President shared that while he continued the Zone Conference that the Spirit whispered to tell me that inspired revelation about my father. Those are the most profound words I've ever heard my Mission President tell me and probably the most profound words I've ever been told in my life.

I'm so grateful for this gospel. And although this is the most difficult situation I've ever been in, I know the Savior will help me and my family overcome this heavy burden. The gospel is true and what glorious truth it proclaims. I'm going to the temple tomorrow to pull myself together.

June 29, 2010

Still recovering quite a bit. A lot of reflecting. The temple was amazing and gave me the strength to get through the day. Got my answer to wait, and I'll know soon whether to go home or stay. Later after talking to my mom, I received the answer that I need to go. I reflected on the beach for a while. I'm really starting to understand how the Atonement of Jesus Christ works in our lives. What a wonderful time in my life to know the truths of the gospel. I'm so grateful for the promises in the temple. I don't know what I'd be doing without the truths I know. I don't know how people cope without the gospel. But I've come to understand that this is where we're tested and tried. And also that this is when the Lord needed my father back. It's hard to accept, but I know his mission here on Earth was completed. That's a promise from the temple. Sounds like I should be able to go home to see the funeral service. But we'll know tomorrow for sure. [I did end up traveling back home for the funeral service and quickly traveled back to my mission in San Diego, California to finish my full two years of service]

August 1, 2010

Wow… What an amazing Sunday. Elder M. Russell Ballard attended our Sacrament meeting! The whole ward thought he had skipped attending this year. But no, he was there. (Elder Ballard vacations in San Diego). So for the first 30 minutes the ward was able to share their testimonies. Which finally gave me a chance to go up and let everyone know about my dad. (since this was my first Fast Sunday back from the funeral). So I went up on the stand and there was one seat next to Elder Ballard that I decided to take. I shook his hand and said "hi". I then went up to share my story about Dad's passing and testimony. Lots of tears, but as I started heading down to my seat from the podium, Elder Ballard grabbed me and asked me to sit next to him. He proceeded to ask me how I've been handling everything and I responded, "well". He asked if I was an English speaking missionary, where I was from, and what my companion's name was. Then it was his turn to share his testimony. Before he said anything, he called my companion, Elder Hartshorn, up to the podium then asked me to come back over next to him. Elder Ballard told Elder Hartshorn and me to put our arms around each other and to find comfort in our companionship. He told us to find, teach and baptize. And he said my dad is doing the same thing on the other side of the Veil. He also told us to read

Doctrine and Covenants 138, because he said that scripture describes exactly what my dad is doing right now.

It was so neat to be up there with Elder Ballard. We then stayed on the stand, but sat down. He then shared his testimony of the gospel. Very simple, but very powerful testimony. Then we sang the closing song and I shared the hymn book with Elder Ballard. It was so cool! Then after the closing prayer, Elder Ballard stood up, gave me a big hug and told me to send his best wishes to my mom. I thanked him for everything, shook his hand one last time and headed to class. Many members came up to me to share their condolences. It was an amazing day and I know my dad got to see all of it.

MEMOIR ON MY FATHER

BY JONATHAN WEHLE, AUTHOR'S SON

Written on November 10, 2014

My dad and I had a very close relationship. We did a lot of dirt bike trips together, scout camps, and long road trips. When I was fourteen and the youngest in the family, my father passed away in Atlanta, Georgia, from a heart attack, while returning home from a business trip. After Dad's Iraq experience, he joined a company with the main office in Atlanta, Georgia. Since Mom and my sister, Cherie (seventeen at the time), were at girls camp, he invited me to accompany him. We had tons of fun, seeing movies, going to the pool in the hotel, and eating out a lot. (Dad's plan on the way home was to pick up a bunch of great fireworks and an anniversary gift for Mom.) At the end of the week and our last day there, we were about to leave for our ten-to-fourteen-hour drive home, but my dad started having some chest pains. Our whole family has always seen my dad as a jokester. For instance, many times at King's Dominion, an amusement park, he would say, "That big ride nearly gave me a heart attack," and we would laugh and tell him to suck it up. But this time was different; I could see it in his eyes. I know Heavenly Father was watching over us, because he started getting chest pains immediately after we were leaving and managed to pull into the parking lot of a doctor's office. I was fortunate enough to help as fast as possible, but before the medical staff was able to do anything, he had already collapsed in one of the waiting room chairs in the building. Within minutes, the ambulance showed up and took my dad to the hospital, while I rode in a police car. It was two hours before the doctor was able to give me the news. Once he did, I felt like everything was falling apart. I asked myself, "How could this happen to me? What did I do to deserve this?" This whole experience was traumatizing for me, considering I was the only one there with him and in a completely different state. One thing I did realize in the midst of all the chaos was that we were in the perfect place for it to happen. The doctor's office was across from his company building, so we never even got onto the highway. If we had been on the road for a while and he suddenly had a heart attack, I might have been killed as well.

I've realized over the years that despite everything that happened to me, I can be thankful because most people don't even get to see their fathers growing up or they pass while they're still a newborn. I'm thankful for being able to have him for fourteen years of my life, even though I never would have guessed I would lose him so early. My mom has told me that she is still able to feel his spirit present during hard times or sudden grieving moments in her life. I'm not sure where I would be if he were still here; my maturity has grown very fast since his death and has given me a different perspective on life.

I received sincere concern from those around me, but it was always, "Sorry about your dad" and nothing else. Then my friends and acquaintances would just continue with their own lives, never really bothering to see me, call me, or give me comfort. I can't blame them; I do understand that they were just kids without a worry in their lives, which is why this really helped me grow in many different aspects of my life.

This experience has taught me that even though we lose our loved ones on Earth, we don't necessarily lose them forever. This gave me the opportunity to conduct my Eagle Project at Dad's burial place, Quantico National Cemetery, where we worked on two memorial stations. Both places got new mulch beds, painted pillars, and ceilings, along with repainted entrance gates. Over time, I started to realize that there would be important moments in my life that Dad would not be there for, like achieving my Eagle Scout rank, graduating high school, getting ordained to the Melchizedek Priesthood, and getting married. In reality, though, during all these instances, he was always there. During my Eagle Scout Court of Honor, practically everyone told me that they felt my father's presence, and nearly everyone teared up to the point that nobody could even speak.

Going to Atlanta with him really changed my perspective on his death. My brother Matthew had eight months remaining on his two-year church mission in San Diego. So, when he got the call from us about Dad's death, it hit him the hardest. He hadn't seen Dad for nearly two years, and the suddenness of the news really tore him apart. I consider myself very fortunate that I was able to have the entire week with Dad, just the two of us. Even though the whole incident was scary, it was easier on me than everyone else. I've learned a lot about being thankful for what we have while we still have it. Being a member of The Church of Jesus Christ of Latter-day Saints doesn't change the fact that when you lose someone, it's heartbreaking. But it does tell you that no matter what, we will see that person again after this life. People don't understand that there is more than this life. Our mortal life is just a fraction of what's to come.

Ten Years After

by Cherie Kaufman,
Author's Daughter

Written on June 28, 2021

There's something about losing my father a decade ago that feels it deserves some reflection. Jon, my husband, missed meeting him by one year and most of my best friends from college don't hear much about him just because it feels like another life. When coming into the new year of 2020, I wasn't thinking about my "resolutions," I was thinking, "Wow . . . ten years ago my life was changed and who I am was shaped forever." How can ten years go so slow and so fast at the same time? This has got to be decade in which I've grown most in my life . . . for a while at least. I've changed a lot for the good, and I've also changed some that I don't love. I actually use "seventeen-year-old me" as an example of who I need to continue to be. Optimistic and faithful—the things that get a little harder the older you get and the more people you lose. My dad taught me all the good things. He was such an example of humility and always made you laugh. He grounded our family in so many ways. I wish so badly everyone could've met him. I'll continue to try and honor him by being a "fix-it girl" around the house (or try to be), riding a dirt bike when I go home (do they even work anymore?), and going on walks at night with my kids to talk about the constellations and the plan of salvation.

EPILOGUE
BY SHARON E. WEHLE,
AUTHOR'S WIFE

How would Mark fill his time after his last trip to Iraq and before his passing? He had his list on his white board. He called it his "Honey-Do List." (I have provided some context in parentheses and italics.)

- Motorcycle repairs and possibly see Matt and Jono bikes, get 4-wheeler working well
- Free firewood in Woodbridge
- Furnace repair (new firebricks)
- Watch Cherie perform at Riverside
- Take Jono to Motocross races in Axton. VA on June 14th
- Dentist for me
- Doctor for me (*He was to have a heart checkup three days after his death and a stress test a week later*)
- Barn estimate
- Heater coils in exhaust flue?
- Garage fun
- Husaberg Engine pulled apart—put dirt bike back together
- New cabinets

- Get rid of all the extra animals that Mom has collected while I'm gone because she is a woman with a soft heart.
- Aerate lawn and fertilize
- Go bowling, movies, laser tag with Jono at Potomac Mills
- Scout Camp with Jono for first half of that week (Jono's heart issues)
- Try to get some quotes for asphalt repairs in driveway
- Go to Utah for Matthew if it all works out.
- Stay home quite a bit and do fun things around the house . . . no all-day shopping trips?
- Continue eating proper and proper quantity and not gain weight back from all that I lost in Iraq
- Play some video games with Jono
- Huggle with my Honey and complain about how everything is a disaster at home because I'm not there to keep everything in line and make myself feel needed!
- Power Wash house
- Celebrate 22 years of Marriage (*not realizing that we had only 2 more years together*).

During those few years at home from Iraq, he was busy with all of the above and more. Both Mark and I were called to be the adult leaders and organize our church youth summer conference, help Matthew with his Eagle Scout project supplying Iraqi elementary students with school supplies, helping and supporting Sharon with church summer girls camp callings, and on and on.

What words are there when your best friend passes, is no longer here physically, no longer here to touch, hug, kiss, walk with, talk with, listen to, pray with, go to activities with, go to the temple, go to the movies with the children, do most everything together with the children, work on the garden together, walk around the property (7 1/2 acres) making plans for the family, making dirt bike trails, jumping on the tramp, shooting off fireworks on the powerline or driveway (really GOOD fireworks), going to church together or missing it sometimes, going to the beach, driving to NYC to see a Broadway play, 911, flying to Utah to take our amazing sons to the MTC as they begin their fulltime missions of two years, seeing the sites of Yellowstone, beautiful Utah sites and all the fun traveling? All those moments—from the special moments of the children's four births with two at home to mundane (yet crazy) daily breakfasts—are unforgettable as we go through this short lifetime of experiences that make us who we are and who we are to become as we make our choices, sometimes good and sometimes not so good, repent, and keep going with the faith that we know there is God's purpose in all things and in all we do.

How can you live over twenty-four years with someone and try to find only a few things that bring you the most joy and happiness that you can share with others as you discuss a life that was so full of service and sacrifice? Did I take for granted Mark and I would grow old together? YES!

Memories include our family prayers together each night, scripture study, our Wehle Circus song when things got crazy, Popcorn Popping Primary song being Mark's favorite song for Family Home Evenings, bonfires, fireworks, throwing the Nintendo against the tree because the kids were arguing (it was old, and he was going to buy a new one anyway), locking David outside when he was little because he was playing too many video games. . . .

Summer 2010 was to be a fun summer of catching up, driving to Palmyra, New York or an amazing church pageant, traveling to the Outer Banks, North Carolina, for our traditional beach trip, and then helping Jonathan with the dirt bikes. None of what we expected to happen would happen that summer. Cherie and I had returned from girls camp and were prepared to get pedicures when we got the call from the Atlanta hospital that Mark's heart could not be stabilized. Surely, he would come out of it, and as Cherie and I knelt in prayer, we were certain things would be okay. We had to be certain. But he did not pull out of it. Cherie stayed home with a friend who comforted her, and I flew to Atlanta to do whatever would be expected, as well as find and comfort Jonathan.

With his Iraqi opportunities, we had paid off our bills and our home, added to our savings, and talked about serving full-time church missions together. How wonderful it would be to be grandparents for our children in our own special way, especially since our children didn't have many opportunities to interact with their own grandparents. The oldest three were married in the year of 2012.

What impressed me about Mark? God had his own time-table with me and meeting my eternal companion. I've always had faith and loved Heavenly Father. I had a very inspired woman answer a question that I always keep in my memory as I courted different young men. I asked her how she knew. How will I know when it's the right man to marry? Her reply was,

"You need to marry your best friend and you look for the man that loves Heavenly Father more than anyone or anything else, and if so, as his wife, you will be right next to him. You will not be above or below, but by his side."

I was always determined to marry a man who was my best friend. I knew I needed to marry my best friend because of problems I'd seen in my own life growing up with a single, working mom. I'd rather marry right the first time or not marry at all. Maybe the Lord was testing me to see if I would really wait for the right one or maybe Mark just had not been ready to meet me or maybe I wasn't ready.

Mark was such a good friend, and we did everything together. I saw such wonderful attributes in him. One thing that set him apart from all the other guys I had dated is how much he loved the Lord and the gospel. His testimony was strong, and he did not take it for granted.

The timeline of all that has happened is not a coincidence either. Mark passed away on our twenty-fourth anniversary? My belief is that this would not have happened if it was not the right time. Am I ready to let him go? No, but it is not my time-table—it is God's. Like the timetable of getting married—that wasn't my timetable either—I was ready and waiting, but God knew it was to be Mark and that I needed to wait for him.

Can I do this? Of course I can! Am I alone? Of course not! I have Heavenly Father, my wonderful, strong children, and Mark's strong spirit here when I need him and when my children need him. I was told in a priesthood blessing of comfort shortly after his funeral that Mark was worried about us, and he was not prepared to leave so soon, but that now he was happy in the missionary work he was doing and knew we would be protected. He knows I'm strong and the children are strong. He knows we'll be alright. Does that mean it will be easy? No! Are the things that help us to grow easy?

Why is it we don't realize God's hands in our lives until something dramatic happens? I've always seen God's hands in my life day to day. But, in looking back over twenty-four years, I'm reminded how very clear it is that our lives are not made up of coincidences or "by luck" experiences. There is purpose in all things, purpose in life and purpose in death. Continuing to make the right choices and follow that sweet spirit of the Holy Ghost keeps us on the right path, continually growing and perfecting ourselves using Jesus Christ as our example in all things.

Mark was very humble and quiet about sharing his spiritual experiences in Iraq. His experiences in Iraq these past years have probably done more to influence him and me and our family in appreciating each other, our lives, and our testimonies more. I missed him so much, but I knew he was supposed to go to Iraq. His experiences were unforgettable with the people and with God. Mark began writing a book, and David felt inspired to compile all that his father had written and photographed in order to publish it as his dad would have wanted to do. It will be an amazing memorial to someone who shared very little about all the lives he touched due to his humility. Having not been able to serve a full-time mission before marrying, I know he is a missionary in heaven to those good people he met in Iraq who did not have the blessings of hearing the fullness of the gospel on Earth. Maybe that's why Heavenly Father took him early . . . to finish his mission on the other side of the veil. In fact, I know that is what he is doing.

Mark did not share with me how dangerous things really were because he didn't want me to worry. And I would have worried. It wasn't as easy to talk regularly because technology wasn't what it is today. I recall the families we helped with clothes and baby things. A very humble people who appreciated things as simple as whiteboards and markers. Often, we would have phone calls to our home in Virginia from those Iraqi friends checking up on him.

Our goals were to get our home and vehicles paid off and to be able to serve missions together. God's plan was a bit different than we were expecting. I would be able to survive without debt when he passed, and I learned how to survive without him as my companion by my side. It was a dry run when he would leave for months at a time, and I would learn how to run the home and be confident in maintaining it and raising children without him. I'm so thankful we had each other for almost twenty-seven years (counting our few years of dating).

Heavenly Father knows our path, and we must have faith that we will realize it and stay on it no matter what the future may hold—even that which we may not expect. We plan for the best, hope for the best, and accept what God has in store for us, knowing He loves us.

Several weeks after Mark's passing, I attended our stake conference with Jonathan. The announcement was made about the importance of mature adult couples coming forward for missions, and it just hit me so hard that Mark and I would not be able to do that on this Earth like we had discussed so many times. I fought back the tears and almost left. A brother came up to me and with very few words gave me a big hug and testified to me that Mark was doing a more important work, one that he enjoyed on earth—that of missionary work—and that his election was sure. He said the hard part is what I need to do: continue to live in such a way that I will be worthy of being with him. My trial on Earth will be much more difficult than his is now.

The day I returned home with Jonathan after the funeral, I walked into the house and went upstairs to see suitcases still unemptied, shoes ready to be worn, books organized in piles to be read, the closet filled with Mark's suits, and shirts I was accustomed to seeing these past twenty-five or so years, hundreds of ties still hanging, some more special that others especially the white one Cherie made for him with fabric-painted designs just for her baptism. Father's Day gifts still sat out and needed to be put somewhere out of sight—it hurt too much. Walking through the garage is inevitable. His dirt bike is pulled apart in pieces, still waiting for his return. Only he knows where each piece, nut, and bolt go. It was to be his summer project so he could go riding with Jonathan.

Now I know why I needed to learn how to run the home by myself those years Mark was back and forth to Iraq. I also was given a small taste of how hard it was to be away from him for so long. Now I smile because, compared to now, the time away from us was a minute back then. I've already learned how to keep myself busy, so I don't miss him so much. But you can't continue this nonstop. You have to say your nightly prayers, go to bed, sleep with no snoring, no tossing and turning by your partner, then get up each morning. Then you remember. It wasn't a dream. It's reality: your sweetie is not here with you and will not be for a long, long time.

But it isn't forever. And that's because of the Atonement of Jesus Christ, which included His death and resurrection. We too are promised that our bodies will be resurrected after death and that we can live with Him and our eternal family if we do our best to follow Him. The gospel of Jesus Christ and its fullness is found in The Church of Jesus Christ of Latter-day Saints, and it gives us the faith to look beyond the grave and look forward to the next life. With that testimony, I can proclaim the same thing about our Savior and my dear husband together: that he lives!

PHOTO GALLERY
THE AUTHOR'S FIRST TRIP TO
IRAQ, 2004–2005

Mark Wehle served as an engineer in the Navy in the early 80s. During his tour of Guam, he met missionaries and was baptized a member of The Church of Jesus Christ of Latter-day Saints.

Mark and Sharon were married in 1986 in the Mesa Arizona Temple.

Even with a busy school schedule at Brigham Young University in Utah, there was always time for Mark's favorite activity: dirt biking. The Wehle's would move to Virginia in 1990.

In 2004 (and four kids later), Mark was ready to try a new challenging assignment after years of working for General Electric and Penpower.

Before he could reach his assigned location at the PC-1 natural gas power plant near Basra (also called the Khor Al Zubair power station), he had to fly into Kuwait City.

Kuwait is a small emirate nestled between Iraq and Saudi Arabia. It has the largest US military presence in the Middle East. (Photo by Rob Faulkner)

Over 4.6 million people call Kuwait City their home. Foreign nationals constitute 70% of Kuwait's population. (Photo by Bob McCaffrey)

The road from Kuwait City to Basra is a dangerous one. The Olive Security contractors plan the safest route for their convoy.

Various checkpoints are spread out over the land. This is by far the most dangerous part of the journey. No one knows if the many locals on the side of the road are harmless or not.

For miles, Mark and the convoy pass desert sights like this. A woman wearing a niqab walks by the train tracks.

A father and his sons sell bananas on the side of the road in southern Iraq. Note the cart being pulled by a donkey.

The convoy has almost arrived. The sign reads "District of Khor Al Zubair Port Welcomes You."

One of the vehicles was peppered by gunfire on the trip. A scary thought, but not as threatening as the road bombs which plague the area.

Mark with one of the security contractors. Basra would be their home for the next several months.

The PC-1 power plant had suffered many mechanical problems since Saddam's regime. The U.S. government had hired General Electric to help bring it back online.

Mark works in one of the trailers near the plant. Security guards accompanied many of the civilian contractors almost constantly.

The inscription reads "Ministry of Industry, Department of National Electric Power, Shaibah Gas Power Plant."

At the end of the work day, all the foreign contractors would take a convoy to the Shaibah Logistic Base where they could safely eat and rest

Mark grabs some food in the common area inside the base.

An Iraqi chef prepares food for the entire camp.

Entertainment is hard to come by, so the residents play music and talk in the common area.

As the convoy travels to the plant, the little children nearby give the A-OK that they haven't seen any terrorist activity.

Old military equipment rusting in the desert is not an unusual sight for the team.

Smoke plumes into the air ominously. It could be an oil field fire, but the constant explosions that rock the area suggest otherwise.

An oil fire takes over the road near the base. Iraqi crews work overtime to contain it.

The Iraqi people work on repairing the turbines. Mark grows closer with them with each passing day, creating friendships that last a lifetime.

Mark visits an abandoned village nearby. The sign reads "Division of Administration."

Mark has lunch with his Iraqi friends, including Galib, Mohammed
One, Omar, and Tariq. This experience is the biggest highlight from his
time in Iraq. (Faces blurred to protect identities)

A sandstorm approaches the base. The sand and wind would irritate the
eyes, but the cool, cloudy weather would be a welcome change.

Mark standing with Malik, the plant manager. (Face blurred to protect identity)

The inhabitants of Al Zubair enjoy a community soccer game. This is the game that Mark drove past as he was leaving Iraq.

In December 2004, Mark makes it home to spend Christmas with the family. After a well-earned rest, he will fly back to Basra to finish the job.

The gift from Galib: The Winged Lion of Babylon. The earliest version of this symbol is attributed to king Nebuchadnezzar II, and it's possible Daniel the prophet saw the same symbol in his throne room.

Various other items (including the prayer rug) given to Mark or purchased in Kuwait City.

PHOTO GALLERY
THE AUTHOR'S SECOND TRIP TO IRAQ, 2007–2008

The dining facility (DFAC) at Camp Victory, home to military personnel and civilians alike. This is where Mark arrived right after the Baghdad airport.

The Al-Qudas gas-fired power plant is located near Baghdad, the capital of Iraq.

The entrance to Qudas. The workers lived here too, so there was no need for a daily convoy. Occasionally people would travel to the nearby military camps for supplies.

Some of the team: Yousef, Mark, Hussain, Wyatt, Kareem, Paul, and Emad. (Faces blurred to protect identities)

Mark originally wanted this photo as the cover of this book. An artistic interpretation is now found on the cover.

Mark speaking with Iraq's Minister of Electricity, Karim Wahid al-Hasan.

Gordon "the Scottish guy" playing his bagpipes for the camp. (Faces blurred to protect identities)

Jassim in his traditional Iraqi garb.

Jassim's children playing in their home. Mark said this was probably one of the first times an American civilian was able to go inside an Iraqi family's household.

Hungry stray cats and dogs were a usual sight inside the Qudas compound.

Like his time in Basra, Mark made many lifelong friends during his second trip to Iraq. (Faces blurred to protect identities)

There was a lot of pressure on the managerial team. It was a high-profile project being covered by multiple news agencies.

During the first day of Eid al-Adha festival, Muslims slaughter their best livestock to honor Abraham's willingness to sacrifice his son. The meat is then divided up, and some is given to the poor and needy.

A bloody handprint is imprinted on the walls for good luck, and to protect the inhabitants from harm.

The bloody handprint is also said to ward away the evil eye during the festival.

A massive sandstorm rolls into the camp, causing the world to turn into a Mars-like environment.

A gigantic new turbine is prepped for installation. This is Mark's specialty, but the process is still nerve-wracking.

Mark enjoying lunch with Nasir, the site manager for the Iraqi construction company. (Face blurred to protect identity)

Luckily, the interior work and maintenance means a respite from the unrelenting desert sun.

Mark and Wyatt (right) eat lunch in their trailer.

One of the towers where the security contractors stand guard gives a great view of the Al-Qudas power plant.

The stones that Mark kept picking up in the camp. It's possible similar stones were picked up by the Brother of Jared so the Lord could touch them and give light to their ships.

The Iraqis prepare Dolma, which is like a dirty rice made with grape leaves. A big pot of the recipe is flipped upside down on top of flat bread, then everyone digs in with their hands.

Mark enjoying the Dolma. The Iraqis always insist that their friends sit down to eat instead of stand.

For Matthew's Eagle Scout Service Project for Boy Scouts, he gathered thousands of school supplies to be donated to school children in Iraq. Mark would be there to help the supplies reach their destination.

Jassim packs the truck with the supplies so he can take them to his village's school.

Mark poses with Jassim's daughter holding a school binder. These photos were later used in the local newspaper detailing the Eagle project.

The supplies arrive at the school in Tarmiya.

The all-girl's school is happy to receive so many school supplies thanks to Matthew, Mark, and Jassim.

Mark visiting with Emad and his two children.
(Face blurred to protect identity)

A group photo of all the site staff who made the Qudas restoration
project a success.

During his time in Iraq, Mark took a trip to Jordan to visit the ancient city of Petra.

The doorway of the Treasury at Petra. It was carved into the sandstone by the Nabataeans in 200 A.D., and likely began as a temple.

After his visit to Petra, he took time to swim in the Dead Sea before his trip back.

Mark Wehle is buried in the Quantico National Cemetery. Jonathan's Eagle Scout Project consisted of cleaning and improving the grounds and memorial stations near his father's gravesite.

The Wehle family has only grown bigger in 2021, and stories of Grandpa Mark and his untold generosity and bravery will be passed down for generations.

ACKNOWLEDGMENTS
BY DAVID WEHLE

I want to extend my biggest thanks and love to my mother, Sharon, for helping so much with this challenging, rewarding project. Your undying love for your husband made this possible. Big thanks to my siblings Matthew, Cherie, and Jonathan for contributing and giving me feedback (and of course, can't forget Jon, Kristyna, and Katie). Thank you to my sweetheart Elise, and my children who I love so much: Evelyn, William, and Samuel.

Every member of Mark Wehle's family contributed to this book and helped make it a reality. Thank you Aunt Diane, Aunt Elaine, and Uncle Kurt. Thank you Suzanne, Nada, Pete, and Brooke! My family on my mom's side also helped immensely: thank you Aunt Sheila, Natalie, Tara, and Shad!

Big thanks to one of my dad's oldest friends, Andrew Lee, who contributed the portrait photo of my dad. Thank you Abigail Henrie Crow and Cherie for your help on the cover art. Bishop Jeffrey Stokes served us ceaselessly during a time of great need, and our love goes out to him and his family.

A gigantic thank you to all the people who donated to the Kickstarter to bring this project to life. Special thanks to these people who went above and beyond with their contributions: Jordan McAllister, Steven White, Gregory Kent Olson, Helen Smith, Theresa Tompkinson, Kevin Wilson, Cindy Black and Uncle Greg, Eileen Taylor, Mim Kala, Michelle Paul, John and Kristi Sumner, Robert Burdsal, Darrel and Cindy Nickolaisen, Allie Saipa'ia, and Emma Bohman. Thank you so much to all of you, I can't tell how much this means to our family!

ABOUT THE AUTHOR

Mark Wehle is a first-time author with years of engineering experience. His years of reading LDS literature and becoming a leading power-plant expert prepared him for this once-in-a-lifetime memoir. He's also the rare type of engineer who is a master of his craft and also of understanding people and their need for human connection, which is displayed full force in *Mending Mesopotamia*. He passed away on June 28, 2010. He was a faithful servant to his family, friends, church, and country and was an inspiring and loving husband, father, and brother.

CPSIA information can be obtained
at www.ICGtesting.com
Printed in the USA
LVHW100933081022
730248LV00018B/578/J